MW01231761

Known By Our Fruit

*A Study of the Fruit of the Spirit
as Found in Galatians 5:22-23*

F. Wayne Mac Leod

Light To My Path Book Distribution
Sydney Mines, NS CANADA B1V1Y5
www.ltmp.ca

Known By Our Fruit

Copyright © 2012 by F. Wayne Mac Leod

A Special thanks to the proof readers:

Diane Mac Leod, Pat Schmidt

Table of Contents

PREFACE

This is a commentary on Galatians 5:22-23. It is a study of what the Spirit of God wants to do in the life of every believer. The fruit of Galatians 5:22-23 is not the fruit of human effort and discipline. It is the fruit of *God's Spirit*— the evidence of His presence in the life of the believer. Where the Spirit of God is given freedom to work, there is evidence of this in the character of His people. Galatians 5:22-23 looks at the character building work of God's Spirit.

There are other important works of God's Spirit as well. There is much interest in our day in the work of God's Spirit as it relates to empowerment for service. We all want to be used of God to do great things. We have met men and women, however, who seem to be empowered by God but whose personal lives have proven to be far from what God intends. How does God expect me to live? What kind of person does He want me to be? Galatians 5:22-23 teaches us something about God's intentions in this regard. I believe this to be the foundation upon which our ministries and relationships need to be built.

I cannot be the husband or wife God intends me to be if I do not know this character building work of God in my life. I cannot be the pastor or Christian leader God expects if I am not being transformed by the fruit of God's Spirit. The great desire of God is not so much to use us as it is to transform us into the image of His Son.

How many problems in the church would be resolved if only we were to let the Spirit of God produce His fruit in our lives? How the work of God would progress if the world saw the reality of the Spirit's character in the lives of believers.

We cannot describe the fullness of the character building work of God's Spirit in this brief study. We can only hope to get a sense of what God wants to produce in us. I trust that this summary of the fruit of God's Spirit will give you a deeper understanding of this all important work of God's Spirit. May it serve to open eyes to this vital work. May it challenge us to open our hearts more fully to what God's Spirit wants to do in us.

F. Wayne Mac Leod

CHAPTER 1

KNOWN BY OUR FRUIT

> (17) Likewise every good tree bears good fruit, but a bad tree bears bad fruit. (18) A good tree cannot bear bad fruit, and a bad tree cannot bear good fruit. (19) Every tree that does not bear good fruit is cut down and thrown into the fire. (20) Thus, by their fruit you will recognize them. (Matthew 7:17-20)

Something wonderful happened the day I received the Lord Jesus as my personal Savior. Not only were my sins forgiven through the work of Jesus on the cross, but on that same day, I received the Holy Spirit as a seal of the Father's commitment to me and my continued growth in this new life.

> (13) And you also were included in Christ when you heard the word of truth, the gospel of your salvation. Having believed, you were marked in him with a seal, the promised Holy Spirit, (14) who is a deposit guaranteeing our inheritance until the redemption of those who are God's possession—to the praise of His glory. (Ephesians 1:13-14)

The Holy Spirit, whom Jesus promised to send to those who believed in Him (John 14:16-17), sets the believer apart from the rest of the world. It is the presence of the Holy Spirit that makes the believer different from the unbeliever. The apostle Paul wrote in Romans 8:9:

> You, however, are controlled not by the sinful nature but by the Spirit, if the Spirit of God lives in you. And if anyone does not have the Spirit of Christ, he does not belong to Christ. (Romans 8:9)

Notice how Paul told the believers in Rome that if anyone did not have the Holy Spirit he or she did not belong to the Lord Jesus. The Holy Spirit brings spiritual life to the believer. He lives in each believer, bringing them to faith in Jesus Christ and making them more like Christ in character and service.

The Holy Spirit enables the believer to live as God requires. It is not possible for the believer to live the life God requires in the flesh. We can be good, but we cannot be Christ-like. We can live well, but we cannot be righteous. We can be disciplined, but we cannot be holy. Christ-likeness, righteousness and holiness come from the Holy Spirit whom Christ sent. We cannot become what God intended us to be without the Spirit's work in our lives.

Jesus told His disciples in Matthew 7:17-20 that they could recognize a true servant of God by the fruit he or she produced. Some believe that the fruit Jesus speaks about here has to do with results in ministry. When they see an evangelist or Christian pastor who is experiencing great results in ministry, they assume he or she must be close to God. This is not always the case. Take a look at the large and prosperous businesses around you. Many of those who build these businesses have nothing to do with the Holy Spirit. Their prosperity is the result of human wisdom and good business skills. This can also be true in the church. It is possible that the size of your church has more to do with good administration than it does with the work of the Holy Spirit. We cannot assume that just because something is prosperous and success-ful it is the work of God's Spirit. Nor can we assume that just because a preacher has many followers it is the result of the Spirit's work. Remember that the Lord Jesus had very few true followers by the end of His ministry on this earth.

The fruit Jesus is speaking about here has more to do with character than statistics. If you want to know whether someone is truly from God, then you need to examine his or her character. If the Holy Spirit lives in the heart of an individual there will be evidence of His presence in their attitude and actions.

It is true that none of us perfectly demonstrate the character of the Lord Jesus. The Holy Spirit has not yet finished His work in us. Believers can resist or grieve the Holy Spirit (see Ephesians 4:30). We do this each time we refuse to let Him deal with sins that separate us from our Lord. If we are not seeing increasing evidence of the fruit of God's character in our lives, however, we need to seek the Lord about this. It is the desire of God to shape us into the image of His Son.

As we examine our lives, there should be evidence of the fruit of God's character developing in us. We should be careful, however, not to mistake human effort for the fruit of God's Spirit. There are several important points we need to make about this.

CHARACTER TRAITS THAT LOOK LIKE THE FRUIT OF THE SPIRIT

Throughout the history of the church, men and women of faith have disciplined themselves in an attempt to become more Christ-like and to demonstrate a deeper measure of the fruit of the Holy Spirit. It is important for us to understand, however, that even the unbeliever, who does not have the Holy Spirit, can discipline himself or herself in human strength to show more patience or kindness. It is possible to train ourselves to be more loving and gentle with people around us. While many people may demonstrate Christ-like characteristics, these characteristics are not necessarily the result of the work of the Holy Spirit in their lives.

In North America the biggest selling books are self-help books that teach how you can become a better person. Countless seminars and conferences are held each year teaching people how to tap into their own strength and become a better person. As wonderful as the results may be, they are not necessarily the fruit of the Spirit, but the result of disciplining the flesh or changing the thought patterns of the mind. Even the unbeliever, who has no part of the Holy Spirit, can change his or her ways and become a better person.

NATURAL CHARACTER STRENGTHS

There was a time when I wrestled with a lack of joy and peace in my life as a believer. In part, this was because I compared myself to others. By nature, I generally have a fairly even emotional life. I don't experience great highs or great lows. Every once in a while I would see a believer who seemed to be more joyous than me. I wondered what was wrong with me because I didn't experience joy in the same way. We need to understand that the expression of the joy of the Lord or the peace of God is different in each one of us. We will not all demonstrate the fruit of God's Spirit in the same way. Our personalities are very different. Some people seem to have a naturally joyous and bubbly personality. Others are more serious and reserved.

Both believers and unbelievers were created in God's image. While that image is tarnished by sin, it still comes through in different forms. You can see something of the artist in the art he or she produces. In a similar way, we can see evidence of the character of God in His creation. This is very evident in nature but it is also evident in the lives of men and women around us as well. It should not surprise us that even the unbeliever demonstrates elements of his or her Creator.

When we see unbelievers demonstrate Christ-like characteristics, we need to be reminded of the One who created them. They are proving that they were created in the image of God. Elements of that image, however tarnished they may be, are shining through. While we may show evidence of the personality of our Creator, these characteristics are not necessarily the fruit of God's Spirit. Even animals demonstrate kindness or love. They reflect something of the character of their Creator, but do not produce the fruit of God's Spirit.

DISTINGUISHING SALVATION FROM THE FRUIT OF GOD'S SPIRIT

None of us will be saved on the basis of how much of the fruit of God's Spirit we demonstrate in our lives. Our salvation is based purely on the work of the Lord Jesus on the cross. We may die before we are able to become

all God intended us to be and still be assured of salvation. Once our salvation is secured, however, the Spirit of
God begins to work on our character, shaping us into the
people the Father wants us to be. The result of His work
is the fruit of the Spirit.

In the chapters that follow we will examine the various
fruits of the Holy Spirit as seen in Galatians 5:22, 23,
seeking to understand what they ought to look like in the
life of the believer. Each of these fruit merits a whole
book in itself. Our goal is to simply introduce the great
character building work of God's Spirit. None of us will
demonstrate all this fruit in perfection. We will quickly
discover our strengths and weaknesses. I would encourage the reader to take the time to examine his or her life
in light of what the Scripture teaches about the fruit of the
Holy Spirit. Ask God to show you your weakness. Ask
Him to produce a greater measure of His character in
you. My prayer is that this study will challenge us to allow
the Spirit of God to produce the character and attitude of
Christ in us in greater measure.

For Consideration:

- Why did the Lord send the Holy Spirit to dwell in
  the lives of His children? What is the work of the
  Holy Spirit in the life of the believer?
- What is the difference between human effort to be
  a better person and the fruit of God's Spirit in our
  lives?
- What changes have you noticed in your Life since
  you came to know the Lord Jesus and were
  sealed by His Holy Spirit?

For Prayer:

- Ask the Lord to show you, over the course of this brief study, the areas of your life He wants to develop in you.
- Thank the Holy Spirit that He has come to build Christ's character in you. Ask Him to forgive you for times you resisted His purpose for your life.
- Ask the Holy Spirit to give you grace to surrender to His work in your life. Pray that the fruit of the Holy Spirit would be more evident in you.

CHAPTER 2

LOVE

The first fruit mentioned in this passage is love. In our day there are many different understandings of love. The best way to understand what Paul speaks about in Galatians 5:22 is to examine how the word is used in the rest of Scripture. The Greek word used here is the word "*agape*." A quick examination of the use of this word in the New Testament should give us a better understanding of this particular fruit. Let's take a moment to see what the New Testament teaches us about agape love.

AGAPE LOVE COMES FROM GOD

Jesus' prayer for His disciples in John 17 has something important to teach us about agape love. Listen to what He says in John 17:26:

> I have made you known to them, and will continue to make you known in order that the love you have for me may be in them and that I myself may be in them.

Notice the phrase *"that the love you have for me may be in them."* We cannot miss what Jesus is saying here. As He prays for His disciples, He is asking God to put *His* love in their hearts. The love Jesus wanted His disciples to have was not their own love. He asked the Father to give His disciples a love that was divine in nature. This was the work of the Holy Spirit.

This same thought is repeated by Paul in Romans 5:5:

> And hope does not disappoint us, because God has poured out His love into our hearts by the Holy Spirit, whom He has given us.

Notice that God pours out *His* love into our hearts by the Holy Spirit. The love Paul speaks about is not human love. It comes from God through the work of His Holy Spirit.

In Romans 15:30 Paul speaks of this love as being the love of the Spirit.

> I urge you, brothers, by our Lord Jesus Christ and by the love of the Spirit, to join me in my struggle by praying to God for me.

The love Paul speaks of here is a love that comes from God through the Holy Spirit who lives in us. It is not a human love.

The capacity to love is in every one of us. Even those who have nothing to do with God can love with human love. Paul speaks here, however, about a love that is the result of the Spirit's work in our lives. We must distinguish the natural love all humans and animals can experience from the love that comes as a work of God's Spirit in our lives.

AGAPE LOVE IS SACRIFICIAL LOVE

One of the first things we notice in a study of *"agape"* love is that this love is a sacrificial love. Jesus reminds us in John 15:13 that the most powerful demonstration of agape love is that a person would lay down his or her life for another.

> Greater love has no one than this, that he lay down his life for his friends.

Agape love is stronger than the desire for self-preservation. Agape love is willing to make the ultimate sacrifice for the one it loves. To lay down one's life in death may be the ultimate sacrifice but it is not the only sacrifice agape love is willing to make. Agape will sacrifice time, money, pride, comfort or whatever is necessary for the sake of the one it loves.

What is special about agape love is that it shows no distinction between friend or foe. It loves both with the same depth of love. It will lay down its life for a friend but will also do the same for an enemy. Jesus is the clear example of this.

> But God demonstrates His own love for us in this: While we were still sinners, Christ died for us. (Romans 5:8)

Jesus loved us even though we were sinners. God did not look at us and find us attractive. In fact, the opposite was true. When the Lord God looked at us, He found us repulsive. He hated the sin that filled every corner of our lives. Listen to what God saw when He looked at the earth in the days of Noah:

> (6:5) The LORD saw how great man's wickedness on the earth had become, and that every inclination of the thoughts of his heart was only evil all the time. (6:6) The LORD was grieved that He had made man on the earth, and His heart was filled with pain. (Genesis 6:5-6)

God was not attracted to what He saw when He looked into the heart of man. His heart was evil. Every inclination of his heart was contrary to God. This grieved God so much that He wished He had never created man. God's heart was filled with pain as He saw how evil had captured humankind.

It was agape love that moved God to reach out and touch those who had rebelled against Him. They had cursed His name and broken His law. They turned their backs on their Creator. God sent His Son to die for them. Jesus died at the hands of rebels. He died with men spitting on Him and cursing His name. There was nothing attractive about these men, but God loved them anyway. Agape love sacrifices itself for its enemies. This love must come from God because it is not natural to our human flesh.

Agape love will willingly deny itself so that a brother, sister or even an enemy will be blessed.

> If your brother is distressed because of what you eat, you are no longer acting in love. Do not by your eating destroy your brother for whom Christ died. (Romans 14:15)

Agape love is more concerned about a brother or sister than self. When a brother is distressed about the type of food we eat, if we love him with agape love, we will be stop eating that food for his sake. Agape love will minister to a husband or wife when tired. It will reach out in compassion and concern and willingly sacrifice all. It will discipline itself and give and give and give. It does this simply because it is the love of God.

AGAPE LOVE DOESN'T CHANGE

Another thing we need to understand about agape love is that it does not change with circumstances. The story of the Prodigal Son in Luke 15 is a good example of this. This son left home with his inheritance and turned his back on his God and his father. He lived a wild life and wasted all his money. He returned home with nothing. The wonderful thing about this story is that the father's love for the son had not changed. The father embraced his rebellious son and restored his position in the family even though he had shamed him.

You can run as far away from God as you can possibly run and God will not love you any less. You can be as faithful to God as you can possibly be and God could not love you more. There is nothing that can separate us from the agape love of God.

> (8:35) Who shall separate us from the love of Christ? Shall trouble or hardship or persecution or famine or nakedness or danger or sword? ... (8:37) No, in all these things we are more than conquerors through Him who loved us. (8:38) For I am convinced that neither death nor life, neither angels nor demons, neither the present nor the future, nor any powers, (8:39) neither height nor

depth, nor anything else in all creation, will be able to separate us from the love of God that is in Christ Jesus our Lord. (Romans 8:35-39)

This is a wonderful thought. No demon in hell, no trial or tribulation, nor anything that I do or don't do in life will change God's wonderful agape love for me. I can be assured of that love forever.

It is relatively simple to love those who are easy to get along with but when we have been hurt by those individuals, our human love quickly turns to anger, bitterness and hatred. Agape love loves those who do us evil as much as it loves those who treat us well:

If you love those who love you, what reward will you get? Are not even the tax collectors doing that? (Matthew 5:46)

According to Jesus, what distinguished His love from our own human love is that His love remains as strong for those who are close to us as it does for those who treat us with evil and contempt. Those who love with agape love bless those who curse them. Agape love turns the other cheek and loves in return for evil. Agape love does not change. No matter what you do it always responds in love. Jesus blessed those who crucified him. Stephen blessed those who stoned him. Agape love never seeks an excuse for not loving—it always loves.

AGAPE LOVE IS MOTIVATIONAL LOVE

There is one more thing we need to understand about agape love. Agape love is motivational love. In other words, agape love controls and shapes the actions we take. If you love with agape love, you will be propelled into action by that love. You will not be able to stop yourself. Listen to what Paul tells us about Christ's love in 2 Corinthians 5:14:

> For Christ's love compels us, because we are convinced that one died for all, and therefore all died.

The word "compel" is a strong word. It means to be pressed in on all sides. It is what happens when a ship is forced into a narrow channel. It is also used to describe a prisoner confined to a cell. Let's open this up further.

When you are pressed in on all sides you have no direction to go but in the direction of the force that is pressing down on you. This is what the agape love of God is like. It presses us in on all sides and shapes our actions. Like the ship being forced into a narrow channel, this love directs and focuses our attention so that we respond according to its prompting. I am a prisoner to this love. It motivates my actions and pushes me to do things that I would not do by natural human choice.

I know that I am demonstrating agape love when I am being compelled by that love to move into action. I know I am being compelled and moved by that love when I find myself loving those I would not normally love in a sacrificial and self-denying way.

PAUL'S DEFINITION OF LOVE

Paul describes the agape love of God in 1 Corinthians 13. While this passage merits a very thorough study, we can only briefly touch on it here.

(13:4) Love is patient, love is kind. It does not envy, it does not boast, it is not proud. (13:5) It is not rude, it is not self-seeking, it is not easily angered, it keeps no record of wrongs. (13:6) Love does not delight in evil but rejoices with the truth. (13:7) It always protects, always trusts, always hopes, always perseveres. (1 Corinthians 13:4-7)

Let me make a few brief comments on these verses.

What Love Is (1 Corinthians 13:4)

Paul tells us two things about agape love in 1 Corinthians 13:4. Love is both patient and kind. It is quite easy to be patient and kind to those who are kind and patient with us. Remember, however, that agape love shows no partiality. It loves those who are kind as much as it loves those who mistreat and abuse. Agape love is patient with those who are difficult and hard. It repays evil with kindness. This is what the Lord God did for us. When we were sinners He showed great patience and kindness toward us. His love in us will do the same for others.

What Love Is Not (1 Corinthians 13: 4-6)

Having told us what love is, Paul now tells us what it is not. Love does not envy. Instead it rejoices in God's blessing in the lives of others.

Agape love is not boastful or proud. The boastful and proud are self-centered. Agape love is focused on others. It delights to serve and minister to the needs of a brother, sister or even an enemy.

This same thought is reflected in Paul's statement about love not being rude or self-seeking. When we are rude we act in a way that does not consider the interests of another. This is not the characteristic of agape love. Agape love takes into consideration the good of others. It seeks to bless and not harm those it loves.

God's agape love is not easily angered. Instead it is understanding and patient with the shortcomings of others.

This love does not keep a record of wrongs. No amount of insults or offenses can keep it from loving. Agape love is not a selective. It loves the one who is kind and generous as much as the one who insults and offends. It forgets offenses.

God's love does not delight in wrong. It is grieved when even an enemy suffers. Agape love does not say: "It serves them right; they had it coming to them." It is pained by the suffering of its fellow human being.

Agape love does not rejoice in evil and judgment, but stands firmly behind truth and righteousness. Because Agape love is God's love it experiences godly sorrow over those who suffer, but it will never compromise the way of truth and holiness.

What Love Always Does (1 Corinthians 13:7)

Paul concludes his definition of love by reminding us what love always does. First, agape love always protects. It will sacrifice its time, effort, resources and even its life for the sake of others. Like a shepherd caring for his sheep, agape love will risk all to protect and care for those it loves.

This love also trusts. There are people we simply cannot trust in this life. They have proven that they are not reliable or trustworthy. The question we need to ask here is who is the object of love's trust? Surely it cannot be the one who consistently disappoints. It seems more reasonable to assume that God is the one in whom agape love always trusts. The one who loves continues to trust in God for the one it loves. Maybe the one you love is going through a difficult time. You feel helpless and nothing you do seems to make a difference. What does agape love do in this situation? It brings that person to the Lord and trusts Him with their life. It does not give up praying and committing them to the Lord. It trusts Him with the one it loves.

Love always hopes. This hope is in God on behalf of the individual but it is also a hope for the one it loves. To hope is to seek the best for someone. It is to see their potential and encourage them to reach out to achieve that potential. Hope not only sees the potential in the worst sinner but also encourages them to achieve that potential.

When everything else fails, agape love perseveres. It will not cease to love when offended. It will not cease to love because the person it loves keeps falling into sin and evil. True love will not give up. It will always persevere.

THE FRUIT OF LOVE IS THE EVIDENCE OF TRUE FAITH (JOHN 13:35)

Let me conclude with one final verse of Scripture.

> By this all men will know that you are my disci-
> ples, if you love one another. (John 13:35)

I trust that I have somehow been able to communicate that the fruit of love is not something that is natural to us. This love is the work of God's Spirit in our lives.

When the world sees that we love those who are unlove-ly, they know that we love with a love that is not of this earth. When they see how we love those who hate and oppress us, they will know that the Holy Spirit is in us. There is no other explanation for this love. The only way you can explain agape love is that God is working in us. To love in this way is not human. To love in this way we must be empowered by God. This love is the fruit of the Holy Spirit who lives in us. When the world sees this love, they know we are Christians because they see the evidence of His love in our lives. Agape love is a powerful witness to the reality of Jesus.

For Consideration:

- What is the difference between human love and the love of God in us?
- Have you seen evidence of God's love in your life?
- Take a moment to write down some of the charac-teristics of God's love we have mentioned in this chapter. Is this the kind of love you are seeing in your life?
- How does the love of Christ in your life motivate you? What is the practical evidence of God's love in your life?

- What keeps you from experiencing this kind of love in your life?

For Prayer:

- Are there individuals you have a hard time loving? Ask the Lord to give you grace to love these individuals as He loves them.
- Are there people who have offended you? Do you keep a record of the wrongs they have done to you? Ask the Lord to release you from keeping a record of wrong. Ask God to give you grace to forgive them and forget what they have done.
- Ask the Lord to give you grace to surrender to the Spirit's desire to create the fruit of love in you.
- Take a moment to ask the Lord to forgive you for the times you have not loved as He requires.

CHAPTER 3

JOY

The second fruit mentioned in Galatians 5:22-23 is the fruit of joy. Joy is difficult to define. The Greek word generally refers to cheerfulness in outlook, a gladness of heart, or a calmness of spirit. Let's take a moment to consider what the New Testament has to teach us about the fruit of joy.

PRIOR TO PENTECOST

As I prepared to write this chapter, I did a study of the use of the Greek word *"xara"* (joy) and how it was used in the New Testament. I was struck by the fact that prior to the coming of the Holy Spirit the word was generally used to refer to the response of the heart to happy situations.

We see, for example, the response of the wise men when they saw the star that would direct them to the baby Jesus.

> When they saw the star, they were overjoyed. (Matthew 2:10)

This star represented hope for these wise men. It would show them the place where the Savior of the world would be found. This was a happy situation that called for rejoicing.

The same is true when the news of the birth of Jesus reached the Shepherd's ears.

> But the angel said to them, "Do not be afraid. I bring you good news of great joy that will be for all the people. (Luke 2:10)

The happy news of a Savior's birth was news of great joy. It brought them hope.

In the Gospels there are many other occurrences of the word joy, usually signifying a happy event. In Luke 10:17 the disciples returned from their short term mission trip rejoicing because they had seen the power of God being demonstrated in their ministry. There was great joy in the hearts of the women who came to the tomb when they heard the angel tell them that the Lord Jesus had risen from the dead (Matthew 28:8). The disciples returned to Jerusalem with a rejoicing heart after they saw the ascension of the Lord Jesus into heaven (Luke 24:51). Even in heaven there is great joy over one sinner who repents of his sin (Luke 15:7-10).

JESUS SPEAKS ABOUT A FULLER JOY

The other striking thing we discover in a study of the New Testament use of the word *"xara"* (joy) is found in the teaching of Jesus. In the Gospels, the Lord Jesus spoke about a joy that was fuller and deeper than what His followers were experiencing. The joy they understood was to some extent dependent on circumstances. Jesus told His disciples, however, that the day was coming when they would receive a joy that could not be taken from them.

> So with you: Now is your time of grief, but I will see you again and you will rejoice, and no one will take away your joy. (John 16:22)

As we have already seen, the joy the disciples experienced to that point seemed to come and go. This was not the type of joy Jesus was telling them about in John 16:22. This was a joy that would never leave. It was not dependent on circumstances or what they were experiencing at the moment.

Jesus went on to tell the disciples in John 16:24 that the day was coming when their joy would be complete.

> Until now you have not asked for anything in my name. Ask and you will receive, and your joy will be complete.

Jesus use of the word "complete" indicates that the joy the disciples were experiencing now was not full. There was a day coming when Jesus' disciples would experience a different kind of joy. This joy is described as a complete (or perfect) joy.

When Christ prayed for His disciples in John 17:13, He asked the Father that they would have a *full measure* of *His* joy in them.

I am coming to you now, but I say these things
while I am still in the world, so that they may have
the full measure of my joy within them.

Again, the joy His disciples were experiencing to that
point was not complete. They experienced joy in small
ways but it was not what the Lord intended them to have.
He spoke of a fuller joy that His father would give them.

Notice that that the source of this joy is the Father
through the Son. The type of joy Jesus was speaking
about was not merely a happiness one would experience
when something good happens to us. It is a gift from
God, a particular work of the Holy Spirit in our lives.

This fullness of joy was not yet theirs because the Holy
Spirit had not yet come. The joy the Lord was speaking
about is the fruit of the Holy Spirit. It was a deeper and
fuller joy. It was a joy that could not be taken away from
them.

THE FULLNESS OF JOY

As we have said, the joy Jesus asked the Father to give
His disciples would be a complete and full joy. It is very
interesting to see the difference in the New Testament
use of the word joy after the coming of the Holy Spirit at
Pentecost. With the coming of the Holy Spirit, their joy
would be very different.

What is particularly striking from the book of Acts to the
book of Revelation is that joy no longer has anything to
do with circumstances. After the coming of the Holy
Spirit, believers experienced joy even in the midst of
severe trials and tribulation. There are many passages

that speak of this. In Acts 13, for example, Paul and Barnabas were preaching in the region of Antioch. The Jews of that region incited the God-fearing women and leading men to persecute them, forcing the apostles to leave the region. They left with great joy in their hearts:

> (50) But the Jews incited the God-fearing women of high standing and the leading men of the city. They stirred up persecution against Paul and Barnabas, and expelled them from their region. (51) So they shook the dust from their feet in protest against them and went to Iconium. (52) And the disciples were filled with joy and with the Holy Spirit. (Acts 13:50-52)

Notice particularly that the disciples were *"filled with joy and with the Holy Spirit."* This joy was the work of the Holy Spirit in their lives. He filled them with joy in the midst of persecution. This was not natural; it was the evidence of God's Spirit working in them.

Paul commended the Corinthians in 2 Corinthians 8:2 because of the overwhelming joy they experienced in the midst of extreme poverty and severe trials:

> Out of the most severe trial, their overflowing joy and their extreme poverty welled up in rich generosity.

Humanly speaking, there is no connection between joy and severe trials or extreme poverty. This, however, was the experience of the Corinthian believers. Despite their situation, they overflowed with joy. Again, this was a clear evidence of the presence of God's Holy Spirit producing the fruit of joy in the midst of trials and afflictions.

The Thessalonians also experienced this wonderful joy in the midst of severe suffering. Writing in 1 Thessalonians 1:6 Paul says:

> You became imitators of us and of the Lord; in spite of severe suffering, you welcomed the message with the joy given by the Holy Spirit.

It is significant to note that the joy these believers experienced was given to them by the Holy Spirit. The circumstances they were living in were described as "severe suffering." This is not the soil in which human joy can grow. Human joy disappears in the midst of suffering and pain. What we are seeing here is the direct result of the ministry of the Holy Spirit in the lives of these New Testament believers.

The writer to the Hebrews speaks of believers who joyfully accepted the confiscation of their property. Writing in Hebrews 10:34 he says:

> You sympathized with those in prison and joyfully accepted the confiscation of your property, because you knew that you yourselves had better and lasting possessions.

Again, we see how the joy spoken of after the coming of the Holy Spirit is radically different. This joy is a fuller and more complete joy. It is a joy that terrible circumstances cannot take away. It is a joy that does not depend on circumstances.

James calls us as believers to consider it pure joy when we face trials of all kinds. Listen to his challenge in James 1:2:

Consider it pure joy, my brothers, whenever you face trials of many kinds.

How is it possible to consider trials pure joy? This is not possible in human strength. The joy James speaks about here is a joy that is foreign to all that is human. It is a joy that only comes through the ministry of the Holy Spirit in our lives.

JOY: A NECESSARY PART OF MATURITY

As we examine the teaching of the New Testament about joy, we soon discover that joy is a necessary part of Christian maturity. It was, in fact, a particular focus of the apostle's ministry.

The apostle Paul makes an amazing statement about the Christian life in Romans 14:17-18. Listen to how he defines the Kingdom of God:

(17) For the kingdom of God is not a matter of eating and drinking, but of righteousness, peace and joy in the Holy Spirit, (18) because anyone who serves Christ in this way is pleasing to God and approved by men.

Paul tells us here that the Kingdom of God is not about rules but about righteousness, peace and joy in the Holy Spirit. Notice that this joy is in the Holy Spirit. Again it is not human joy but spiritual joy.

Joy in the Holy Spirit is an essential part of what the Christian faith is all about. We understand that the kingdom of God is about righteousness and peace with God, but do we really believe what Paul is telling us about the kingdom of God also being about joy in the Holy Spirit?

We have all been in churches where joy is the last thing we would expect to find. How important is joy in the Christian life? Paul's statement in Romans 14:17-18 is significant. He tells us that we have not truly understood the Kingdom of God if we do not understand the joy that His kingdom brings.

Paul was so convinced of the importance of joy in the Christian life that he told the believers in 2 Corinthians 1:24 that this was one of his purposes in working with them:

> Not that we lord it over your faith, but we work with you for your joy, because it is by faith you stand firm.

Paul wanted to stay with the Philippians so that they would progress in their experience of joy in the faith.

> Convinced of this, I know that I will remain, and I will continue with all of you for your progress and joy in the faith (Philippians 1:25)

We understand from these verses that the apostles believed that a joyless Christian was an immature Christian. Paul made it his goal to see the believers he worked with walked in the joy of the Holy Spirit.

There are many believers who need to examine this teaching of Scripture more closely. A joyless church is an immature church. The prayer of Jesus was that all believers would have a joy that was full. The apostles took this matter seriously and prolonged their stays in villages where they worked so that the believers would know this joy. Maybe as pastors and Christian leaders we would do well to make this our goal in ministry -- not only to experience this joy in the Lord but lead those God has given us to shepherd into the experience of this joy.

Paul challenges the church in Colossae to give thanks to God with joy.

> (11) being strengthened with all power according to his glorious might so that you may have great endurance and patience, and joyfully (12) giving thanks to the Father, who has qualified you to share in the inheritance of the saints in the kingdom of light. (Colossians 1:11-12)

God wants us to experience great joy because of what He has done for us. Joyless worship is not true worship. When it comes to giving thanks to the Lord God we are to do so with joy in our heart. The same is true when it comes to offering or gifts to God. Paul tells us that God expects us to give with a cheerful or joyful heart.

> Each man should give what he has decided in his heart to give, not reluctantly or under compulsion, for God loves a cheerful giver. (2 Corinthians 9:7)

We do God no honor if we do not give Him our offerings with joy in our hearts. We do Him no honor if we do not season our worship with joy. We do not serve God as we ought if we do not serve Him with joy. Imagine that every time you received a gift from someone he or she complained about how much it cost and let you know that it was a bother to give you the gift. Would you not prefer that this person keep their gift? If we want our worship or our gifts to be accepted, they must come from hearts of joy.

Joy is a necessary part of Christian maturity. If your Christian faith is joyless you need to seek the Lord about it. If you are not experiencing joy, you need to ask God why this important fruit of His Spirit is not being produced in you as it ought to be.

THE CAUSE OF JOYLESSNESS

What is the cause of joylessness in the Christian walk? To answer this question properly I would need to write another book. For our purposes here, however, I would like to make two simple comments.

Misunderstanding

The first cause of joylessness in the Christian life has to do with a misunderstanding of the importance of joy. There are believers who are very uncomfortable with too much joy in worship or service of the Lord. They are afraid that if we enjoy our worship or service too much we risk worshipping or serving for ourselves and not for God.

Once again we need to understand that unless we worship and serve with joy in our hearts we are not worshipping and serving the Lord as we ought. God expects that we be joyful in worship and service. Joy is a fruit of the Spirit. If we are not experiencing joy in our Christian walk we are not living as Christ expected. Jesus prayed that we would experience complete and full joy. The apostles believed in the importance of seeing joy in the lives of their converts. Paul taught that the Kingdom of God was about righteousness peace and joy in the

Holy Spirit. Joy, as a fruit of the Holy Spirit, is not an
option. If you want to become everything God calls you to
be, you must make it your heart's desire to experience
His joy.

What a powerful witness it is to the Lord when God's
people are filled with the fruit of joy in every circumstance. A joyless Christianity is not an attractive Christianity. A joyless Christianity is not a mature Christianity.

Disbelief

There is an important passage in Romans 15:13 that
speaks to this issue of joy and the reason for joylessness
in our life.

> Now may the God of hope fill you with all joy and
> peace in believing, that you may abound in hope
> by the power of the Holy Spirit. (NKJV)

Paul's prayer is that God would fill the Christians with joy
in believing (NKJV). We may understand the importance
of joy in the Christian life, but continue to lack joy because of unbelief. Unbelief or lack of trust (NIV) is the
enemy of joy. We will be filled with joy as we believe and
trust the Lord in faith.

Is it possible to believe that Jesus has saved us from our
sin and not experience joy? Is it possible to believe that
we are destined for an eternity with our Lord in heaven
and not sense joy well up within? It is possible to believe
that God works out every situation in life for our good and
not smile with delight no matter what the enemy throws at
us? Is it possible to experience intimacy with the Holy
Spirit and not know joy? You see, unbelief can keep you

from experiencing the joy of the Lord. Only when you find yourself doubting God's provision and salvation can that joy be taken from you. You are filled with joy as you believe and trust in what He has said in His Word. If you are not experiencing the joy of the Lord, you may need to deal with unbelief.

Let me make a brief comment here as one who has suffered from chronic depression. There were a number of years in my life when there was no song in my heart. This was not the result of unbelief. In fact, it was my belief in Christ that got me through those years of depression. I remember a friend of mine attending a Bible study I was doing at the time. After I had completed the Bible study he came up to me and said:

"Wayne, I saw you when you came into the room. You looked so down, but as you began to lead the Bible study, I literally saw you change. By the end of that study your face was different. I saw the light in you again."

Our minds and our bodies are affected by the result of sin in the world. Mental illness is the fruit of living in a sin cursed earth just as all sickness and disease is. Many of God's people experienced bouts of depression and were overwhelmed by the struggles of this world. Certainly, this did hinder their experience of the fullness of joy, but the Spirit of God continues to work. When that joy comes in the midst of depression, it is clearly from God.

Take a moment now to ask yourself if you are experiencing the joy that Paul speaks about as a fruit of the Holy Spirit. This is a joy that is full and complete because it is stronger than any trial or circumstance that can come our way. Ask yourself if that joy is being demonstrated in your service of the Lord? If not, ask the Lord to give you a deeper experience of His joy. What a difference it makes when we open our heart to the work of the Holy Spirit and allow Him to produce His joy in us. Our worship is changed. Our service is changed. Our testimony is powerful. If we are to become the people God has called us to be, we need Him to produce the fruit of joy in our lives.

For Consideration:

- What is the difference between human joy and joy that is the fruit of God's Spirit?
- How do trials affect human joy? Is the Spirit of God able to produce joy in those same trials?
- What is the connection between joy and maturity in the Christian life? Can we be mature without knowing joy as the fruit of God's Spirit in our lives?
- What is the connection between our belief and the joy of the Spirit?
- What hinders joy in our lives? Do you think that we will always experience all that joy the Lord wants to give us in this life?
- Have you experienced evidence of the Spirit's joy in your life? Explain

For Prayer:

- Ask the Lord to show you if there is any hindrance to fuller joy in your spiritual walk.
- Thank the Lord that He wants us to experience complete and full joy in our relationship with Him.

- Ask the Lord to forgive you for the times you have not been joyous in your spiritual walk and service.
- Thank the Lord that He continues to work on us even when we are not experiencing the fullness of joy He wants to give.

CHAPTER 4

PEACE

The third fruit of the Spirit mentioned in Galatians 5:22 is peace. On a very basic earthly level peace is defined as an absence of spiritual, emotional and physical turmoil. This kind of peace is often connected to our circumstances. We have peace when our circumstances no longer cause us stress. There are several examples of this in the Gospels.

PEACE AT ITS BASIC LEVEL

In Mark 5:34 a woman who had a flow of blood secretly touched the hem of Jesus' clothing. Knowing that healing power had left Him, Jesus sought her out. When He found her, He said:

> "Daughter, your faith has healed you. Go in peace and be freed from your suffering."

Notice the connection between the physical suffering this woman endured and her peace. Her flow of blood had been a constant source of distress. When Jesus healed her, He set her free from that distress and her peace was restored.

There is a similar incident in Luke 7 with a woman who came to wash Jesus' feet. Luke tells us that this woman had lived a sinful lifestyle (Luke 7:37). When she approached Jesus, she stooped down, anointed His feet with perfume and washed them with the tears that rolled down her cheeks. Her heart was deeply troubled. She knew she needed forgiveness, and until she received that forgiveness she could have no peace in her life. Seeing her attitude and repentant heart, Jesus spoke to her in Luke 7:50:

> Jesus said to the woman, "Your faith has saved you; go in peace."

This woman was going through tremendous emotional and spiritual turmoil in her life. She knew she was a sinner. She knew that her life was a mess, and that she was far from God and in desperate need of His touch. She came with deep grief and turmoil in her mind and soul. She washed His feet as a symbol of that humility and repentance. That day Jesus forgave her sins. He told her that her faith had saved her and that now she could be at peace, with God and in her own soul. We see from these verses that peace can be taken from us because of physical affliction or because of a spiritual barrier between us and God.

Scripture also speaks about a peace that is the result of a harmonious relationship between individuals.

> Make every effort to keep the unity of the Spirit through the bond of peace. (Ephesians 4:3)

> Let us therefore make every effort to do what leads to peace and to mutual edification. (Romans 14:19)

> Make every effort to live in peace with all men and to be holy; without holiness no one will see the Lord. (Hebrews 12:14)

Peace will be demonstrated in the way we relate to one another in the body of Christ.

At it very basic level peace is an absence of physical, spiritual, emotional or relational turmoil. The question we need to ask ourselves, however, is whether this absence of turmoil is the fruit of God's Spirit. Even the unbeliever, who does not have the Holy Spirit, can experience peace at this basic level. Is there a peace that comes only as a result of the work of the Spirit of God in our lives?

THE PEACE JESUS GIVES

There is a deeper aspect to peace that only the true believer can experience. One of the reasons the Lord Jesus came to this earth was to bring peace. Zechariah, the father of John the Baptist, speaking of the ministry of the Messiah, tells us that that He came "to shine on those living in darkness and in the shadow of death, to guide our feet into the path of peace" (Luke 1:79). This shows us that there is a special peace that Jesus came to give.

Jesus came to "guide our feet into the path of peace." What is this path of peace? Clearly it has to do with our need of forgiveness and a restored relationship with the Father. As sinners, we were separated from God and His blessings. We were under His judgment and headed for

an eternity under His wrath. Jesus came to bring forgiveness and healing of that relationship. He paid the
price for our sin so that all who believe on Him can
become children of God (John 1:12) and be restored to a
right relationship with God.

There is something incredible about this peace. It is a
deeper peace than anything the world has to offer. What
can compare with the knowledge that I am in a right
relationship with my Creator and that I have a future in
His presence forever. How did this peace come to me?
Were it not for the Holy Spirit, I would never have known
my need of a Savior. Were it not for Him opening my
eyes, I would not have seen the solution to my sins in the
person of the Lord Jesus and His work. Were it not for
Him softening my heart, I would never have surrendered
to Christ and accepted His work on my behalf. I owe this
peace with God to the work of Christ on the cross and the
ministry of the Holy Spirit who applied that work in my life.
This relationship with God forms the basis for the peace
that comes as the fruit of God's Spirit.

PEACE AS THE FRUIT OF THE HOLY SPIRIT

Once we have made peace with God through the work of
the Lord Jesus, the Holy Spirit begins the work of trans-
forming our lives from the inside. He produces His fruit in
our lives. The particular fruit we are examining here is the
fruit of peace. The peace that comes to us as a result of
the work of God's Spirit is not like the peace the world
has. Jesus made this clear in John 14:27 when He said:

> Peace I leave with you; my peace I give you. I do
> not give to you as the world gives. Do not let your
> hearts be troubled and do not be afraid.

There are three principles we need to see in John 14:27.

First, notice that Jesus said: "*my* peace I give you." This phrase tells us something very important about the peace Jesus spoke of here. The peace Jesus speaks about is His peace. It comes from Him, and is given to those who are in a relationship with Him. It is a gift to all who know Him as their Savior.

Second, notice that this peace is not the peace the world gives. The peace Jesus speaks about here is very different from the peace we know in this world. This peace is from God. It will look very different from the peace we have experienced in this world.

Third, notice the phrase, "do not let your hearts be troubled and do not be afraid." This implies that the disciples would have cause for trouble and fear in their lives. The peace Jesus offered was a peace that came not in the absence of trouble but in the midst of trouble.

The peace Jesus offered was a peace that this world could not know. Only His disciples could experience this type of peace because of their relationship with the Father. Let's take a moment to consider what Scripture teaches us about the kind of peace the Lord Jesus offered His disciples as the fruit of His Spirit in their lives.

It does not depend on circumstances

The first thing we see in the Word of God is that peace that is the fruit of the Spirit does not depend on the circumstances that unfold in our lives. Listen to what the Lord Jesus told His disciples in John 16:33:

> I have told you these things, so that in me you
> may have peace. In this world you will have trou-
> ble. But take heart! I have overcome the world.

Jesus is saying that they would have trouble in this world
but they would also have peace. Notice two details in this
verse. First Jesus said that the disciples could have
peace *"in me"* (NIV). In other words, this peace came
because they were in a personal relationship with Him.
Notice also that He reminded them that He had "overcome the world." What does this tell us about the peace
offered here? It shows us that peace comes as a result of
our relationship with Jesus and our confidence in His
work and guidance in our lives. Jesus was showing His
disciples that they were His children and He was their
Protector and Guide. He had overcome the world, and if
He was for them, who could be against them (see Romans 8:31). They could have peace in any circumstance
in life as they trusted in Him and His care. One of the
great works of the Holy Spirit is to lead us into a deeper
confidence and trust in the Lord Jesus and His Word. As
the Spirit of God works in our hearts we will be able to
face difficult situations with confidence in our Lord. We
can have assurance of the Lord's care and provision in
even the most trying circumstances. This increasing
confidence and trust in God is the fruit of peace and the
work of God's Spirit in our lives.

Listen to Paul's prayer for the Thessalonians. He prayed
that they would have peace "at all times" and "in every
way":

> Now may the Lord of peace himself give you
> peace at all times and in every way. The Lord be
> with all of you. (2 Thessalonians 3:16)

"All times" includes the difficult times as well as the good times. The peace Paul prays about here is a peace that can be ours in every situation in life. It can be ours because it is not dependent on circumstances. It is the result of the Holy Spirit's work in our lives drawing us into a deeper trust in the Lord Jesus who has overcome the world.

It brings harmony between God and man

The other aspect of the peace the Holy Spirit brings has to do with our ongoing relationship with God. I am not speaking here about our salvation. I am assuming that this is already a reality. As believers, however, there are many temptations in this world that seek to draw us away from the Lord. While our salvation with God is secure, the fruit of peace can be affected.

Paul reminds us in Galatians 4:6-7 that the Spirit of God comes so that we can understand and appreciate our new found relationship with the Lord as His child:

> (6) Because you are sons, God sent the Spirit of his Son into our hearts, the Spirit who calls out, *"Abba,* Father." (7) So you are no longer a slave, but a son; and since you are a son, God has made you also an heir.

Notice how the Spirit of God calls out "Abba, Father." The ministry of the Holy Spirit is to show us the depth of relationship we now have with God as a Father. As we come to appreciate this relationship with the Lord God, the result is an increasing peace in our lives. We know that as a loving heavenly Father He cares for us. We know that we are His sons and daughters and heirs to all

His blessings. With this as our confidence we can face all that life hurls at us with peace in our heart.

It is the great desire of the Spirit of God to reveal the Father and the Son to us in an ever increasing way. Listen to the words of Paul:

> And we, who with unveiled faces all reflect the Lord's glory, are being transformed into his like-ness with ever-increasing glory, which comes from the Lord, who is the Spirit. (2 Corinthians 3:18)

> I keep asking that the God of our Lord Jesus Christ, the glorious Father, may give you the Spirit of wisdom and revelation, so that you may know him better (Ephesians 1:17)

There is a powerful connection between knowing God and the peace we experience in our daily lives. Our peace is in God and a result of the relationship we have with Him. The Holy Spirit jealously guards this relation-ship. Anything that would hinder our relationship with God will also hinder the fruit of peace. Sin will cloud our relationship with God and our understanding of His purposes. This grieves the Holy Spirit (see Ephesians 4:29-32). As the Holy Spirit works in our lives to produce peace, He will deal with unbelief and sin. His desire is that nothing keeps us from intimacy and knowledge of who we are in Christ. He wants to protect us from any-thing that would hinder the fruit of peace He wants to produce in us.

THE CALL TO PURSUE PEACE

There is a very real sense in which we must cooperate with the Holy Spirit if we want to experience the peace He wants to produce in us. The apostle Peter challenges us in 1 Peter to pursue peace.

> For, "Whoever would love life and see good days must keep his tongue from evil and his lips from deceitful speech. 3:11 He must turn from evil and do good; he must seek peace and pursue it. (1 Peter 3:10)

There are two points we need to see in this verse. First, notice the connection between turning from evil and experiencing peace. Sin and evil are enemies to peace. If we want to know the fruit of peace in our lives, we must be willing to turn from sin.

Notice second in 1 Peter 3:10 that we are called to seek peace and pursue it. To seek is to have a desire for something. We all want peace in our lives. Peter tells us, however, that it is not enough to want peace, we must also pursue it. If we are to pursue peace the verse tells us that we must first deal with evil and sin. Let's consider this for a moment.

What happens when you face a difficult trial in your life? Sometimes we begin to complain or become bitter. This is what happened to the nation of Israel as they wandered through the wilderness. They grumbled about the trials they encountered on the way. This grumbling showed that they did not trust the Lord God. They needed to confess their unbelief and surrender to His purposes for their lives. They needed to realize that He was in control of their situation and would use it to shape them into His image. They had no peace in their wilderness wandering because they were not trusting the Lord or recognizing His leading. The sin of unbelief kept them from the experience of peace.

Often in our Christian walk we do not experience peace because we do not trust the Lord. Am I able to trust God and experience His peace and rest when I do not understand what He is doing? Unbelief and rebellion against His purpose will hinder the peace the Spirit of God wants to create in us. If we want to know the fruit of peace we must learn to trust God and what He is doing.

Acts 7:54-59 is a wonderful example of the ministry of the Holy Spirit producing peace in the life of Stephen. As the religious leaders of the day were stoning him, Stephen looked up into heaven and saw the Lord Jesus seated on His throne. Peace flooded his heart when he saw the Lord. Stephen's face glowed like that of an angel. He could have looked at the injustice of what was happening to him. He could have questioned why God was allowing him to be persecuted. He did not do this. Instead, he allowed the Holy Spirit to reveal Christ to him in his moment of trial. He offered forgiveness to his persecutors. The result was a peace that the world could never know.

Paul told the believers of Colossae to make a conscious decision to allow the peace of God to rule them.

> Let the peace of Christ rule in your hearts, since as members of one body you were called to peace. And be thankful. (Colossians 3:15)

If peace was to rule, they needed to surrender to God and trust His purpose. Notice that Paul tells them that they had been called to peace. This was God's purpose. If they were to experience that peace, however, they would need to actively surrender to God's Word and the work of His Holy Spirit in their lives.

GROWING IN PEACE

Spirit Controlled minds

If peace is a necessary part of Christian maturity, how can I experience this peace and grow in it? Paul teaches us in Romans 8:6 that if we want to know the peace of God, the Holy Spirit must be given control of our minds and thoughts.

> The mind of sinful man is death, but the mind con-trolled by the Spirit is life and peace.

It is quite easy to understand what Paul is speaking about here. How many times have I become worried or anxious about the things I face in life? Fleshly thinking will turn our eyes from the hope and provision we have in the Lord. Very often we do not experience peace because our thoughts are not the thoughts of the Spirit of God. We are not thinking as Christ thought. We are allowing the flesh to control our mind. The mind controlled by the Spirit is at peace because it is a mind that trusts the Lord. If you want peace you will have to turn from your fleshly thoughts and allow the Holy Spirit to control your mind and way of thinking.

Obedient hearts

The Scripture tells us, secondly, that if we want to grow in the fruit of peace we must commit ourselves to walking in obedience. Listen to what Paul told believers in Colossians 3:15-16:

> (3:15) Let the peace of Christ rule in your hearts, since as members of one body you were called to peace. And be thankful. (3:16) Let the word of Christ dwell in you richly as you teach and admonish one another with all wisdom, and as you sing psalms, hymns and spiritual songs with gratitude in your hearts to God.

Notice the connection between letting the peace of Christ rule in their hearts and letting the Word of God dwell in them richly. The Word of God can only dwell in our hearts as we surrender to it and live in obedience. You cannot experience the fruit of peace while grieving the Holy Spirit through disobedience to His Word. If we are to experience peace, we must let God's Word dwell in us through obedience.

Paul repeats a similar thought in Philippians 4:9:

> Whatever you have learned or received or heard from me, or seen in me--put it into practice. And the God of peace will be with you.

As the Philippians chose to walk in obedience to the principles Paul taught them, the God of peace would reveal His peace to them. Again it is quite clear here that if we are to experience the fruit of peace we must commit ourselves to walking in obedience to the Word of God.

Trusting and Believing

In Romans 15:13 Paul shows that there is a connection between peace and trust in the Lord God.

> May the God of hope fill you with all joy and peace as you trust in him, so that you may overflow with hope by the power of the Holy Spirit.

Paul's prayer was that God would fill His people with peace as they trusted in Him. Peace is the fruit of trust and belief in God. It is those who believe God who experience peace. It is those who trust His provision and protection who face the trials of life with peace in their heart. Unbelief is the enemy of peace.

Knowing Christ

Peter tells us that peace is multiplied through the knowledge of Christ.

> Grace and peace be yours in abundance through the knowledge of God and of Jesus our Lord. (2 Peter 1:2)

If you want to know peace you need to know the Lord Jesus. Learn who He is and what He has done for you. Understand the depth of His love and commitment to you, and His sovereign provision and care. If you see Jesus for who He is and trust in Him, you will know peace. The Holy Spirit produces the fruit of peace in us by revealing more of the character and person of Christ.

THE PROMISES OF THE GOD OF PEACE

There are some wonderful promises in Scripture from the "God of peace" to all who belong to Him. If you are worried about the power of the enemy before you, Paul reminds you that the "God of peace" will crush Satan under your feet.

> The God of peace will soon crush Satan under your feet. The grace of our Lord Jesus be with you. (Romans 16:20)

If you feel troubled in your heart, feeling you might not have the strength to do what the Lord has called you to do, let God equip you.

> (13:20) May the God of peace, who through the blood of the eternal covenant brought back from the dead our Lord Jesus, that great Shepherd of the sheep, (13:2) equip you with everything good for doing his will, and may he work in us what is pleasing to him, through Jesus Christ, to whom be glory for ever and ever. Amen. (Hebrews 13:20)

Are you anxious over some matter in your life? Paul tells us that the "peace of God" will guard your heart and mind:

> (4:6) Do not be anxious about anything, but in everything, by prayer and petition, with thanksgiving, present your requests to God. (4:7) And the peace of God, which transcends all understanding, will guard your hearts and your minds in Christ Jesus. (Philippians 4:6-7)

Notice in all these verses that God is referred to as the "God of peace". He is greater than our circumstances. He longs to produce the fruit of peace in your heart. No matter what you face in life, you can know this peace as you allow the Spirit of God to remove the obstacles and point you to the One who alone can give you the fullness of peace.

For Consideration:

- How is peace, as a fruit of God's Spirit, different from the peace the world knows?
- What is the connection between knowing God and peace?
- Scripture teaches that we are to pursue peace. How do we do this?
- What are the promises of the "God of peace" to those who love Him?
- How does sin hinder our experience of peace?
- What is the role of the Spirit of God in producing peace in our lives? How does He do this?

For Prayer:

- Thank the Lord that He wants us to know a peace that this world cannot give.
- Ask the Holy Spirit to reveal anything in you that hinders the fruit of peace in your life.
- Ask God to reveal more of Himself and His character to you. Thank Him that as He does you can know greater peace and security.

CHAPTER 5

PATIENCE

So far in this study of the Fruit of the Spirit we have examined love, joy and peace. We all want to see this fruit in our lives. The fourth fruit, however, is less sought after. I have met individuals who have told me that they have stopped praying for patience, because when they did, the Lord seemed to send them trials.

The word used for patience in the Greek language is the word "*makrothumia*." This word comes from two smaller words ("*makros*" and "*thumos*"). The word "*makros*" literally means "long" or a "long time." "*Thumos*" refers to "fierceness" or "anger." When you put these two words together you get the sense of staying long under fierce or difficult circumstances. Patience is the quality of some- one who is able to endure long periods of trial or testing without giving up. While none of us delights in trials or testing, it is vital that we endure them if we are to become all that God wants us to be. Let's take a moment to consider what the New Testament has to tell us about the fruit of patience.

DEMONSTRATED IN THE WAY GOD DEALS WITH US

Perhaps more than any other apostle, Paul understood the patience of God toward him as a sinner. He writes in 1Timothy 1:16:

> But for that very reason I was shown mercy so that in me, the worst of sinners, Christ Jesus might display his unlimited patience as an example for those who would believe on him and receive eternal life.

Paul believed that the Lord was using him as an example to demonstrate His "unlimited patience."

Before his conversion, Paul persecuted the church. He hated the cause of the Lord Jesus and His followers. God could have judged him for the terrible evil he did to the cause of the kingdom, but instead He was very patient with him. He pursued Paul and won his heart, forgiving him for all his offenses.

Where would we be if it were not for the patience of the Lord toward us? Peter makes it clear that were it not for the patience of the Lord, we would still be in our sin.

> Bear in mind that our Lord's patience means salvation, just as our dear brother Paul also wrote you with the wisdom that God gave him. (2 Peter 3:15)

We owe our salvation to the Lord's wonderful patience. He did not give up on us when we were lost in our sin. He could have destroyed us, but He didn't. He bore with us and reached out to us in our sin and rebellion, drawing us to Himself.

As believers we know this wonderful patience of the Lord toward us in our sin. We often fail our Lord. Our attitudes are not always right. We have turned our backs on Him, choosing our own way. We speak things we should never have spoken. Despite these shortcomings, the Lord continues to love us and be patient with us. He does not give up on us.

PATIENCE IN OUR RELATIONSHIP WITH OTHERS

The New Testament exhorts us, in light of the patience of the Lord Jesus toward us, to be patient with our brothers and sisters. Evidence of the fruit of patience will be seen in how we treat each other. In Ephesians 4:2 Paul challenges believers to be patient and to bear with one another:

> Be completely humble and gentle; be patient, bearing with one another in love.

The Greek word translated as "bearing with" can also mean "put up with," "endure," or "suffer." This implies that the people we are bearing with are not always easy to deal with. This demands a powerful work of God in our lives. Patience is the ability to "endure" people who are difficult to get along with. This is not something that many of us want to do. In fact, it is not natural for us to bear with difficult people. Remember, however, that this is how God has treated us. He has endured our sin and rebellion. If we let Him, the Holy Spirit will produce this kind of patience in us for others.

In Colossians 3:12-13 Paul brings a challenge to the Colossians:

> (3:12) Therefore, as God's chosen people, holy and dearly loved, clothe yourselves with compassion, kindness, humility, gentleness and patience. (3:13) Bear with each other and forgive whatever grievances you may have against one another. Forgive as the Lord forgave you.

Paul uses the same Greek word as he did in Ephesians 4:2, encouraging the believers to "bear with" each other (to "put up with," "endure," or "suffer"). Notice also, however, that he tells them to forgive whatever grievances they may have with each other. This implies that those who they were to be patient with were not only difficult people but people who had offended them in some way. Paul's challenge was to forgive these people and bear with them because this is how the Lord had treated them.

It is relatively easy to be patient with those who are easy to get along with. Paul is asking us to be patient, however, with those who have grieved us. How thankful we need to be that the Lord did not give up on us. He forgave us when we sinned against Him. He bore with us when we were wandering from him. Paul described God's patience toward him as an "unlimited patience" (see 1 Timothy 1:16, NIV). Those who know the fruit of the Spirit's patience will demonstrate this same attitude toward those who have offended them.

The patience Paul speaks about here is a gift from God, the work of His Spirit in our lives. As the Holy Spirit creates this type of patience in us, He will require that we lay down all bitterness and anger against our brother or sister. He will demand that we forgive those who have offended us. The patience God wants to create in us will call for forgiveness and surrender of wrong attitudes. This will not be easy, but it will always be for our good.

PATIENCE IN SUFFERING

The fruit of patience is also demonstrated in the way we handle difficulties and struggles in life. The apostle Paul was a good example of patience in suffering. Notice what he tells us in 2 Corinthians 6:4-6:

> (6:4) Rather, as servants of God we commend ourselves in every way: in great endurance; in troubles, hardships and distresses; (6:5) in beatings, imprisonments and riots; in hard work, sleepless nights and hunger; (6:6) in purity, understanding, patience and kindness; in the Holy Spirit and in sincere love.

The apostle Paul faced much opposition in his ministry. He was beaten and stoned. He was chased out of cities where he preached. People wanted to kill him. He was insulted and falsely accused. He endured much for the cause of the Lord Jesus. In spite of all these things, he was confident that he had left a good example for Timothy, his son in the faith:

> You, however, know all about my teaching, my way of life, my purpose, faith, patience, love, endurance (2 Timothy 3:10)

He never gave up. When he was beaten, he got back up on his feet and continued his mission. He kept going despite the obstacles thrown in his path. This is the quality of one who has patience. He or she is able to bear

the pressure that comes from all sides, remaining under
that pressure without giving up or giving in. This is
because the Spirit of God continues to strengthen and
motivate them in their work. He pushes them on.

PATIENCE: THE SOIL IN WHICH OTHER FRUIT CAN
GROW

Patience is a fruit that not too many of us want because
we do not want the things that often come with it. We
would rather live without difficult people and the testing of
our faith. What we need to understand about patience,
however, is that it is rich soil in which other fruit of the
Spirit can grow. Listen to Paul's prayer for the Colossians:

> (1:11) being strengthened with all power accord-
> ing to his glorious might so that you may have
> great endurance and patience, and joyfully (1:12)
> giving thanks to the Father, who has qualified you
> to share in the inheritance of the saints in the
> kingdom of light. (Colossians 1:11-12)

Notice the connection here between patience and being
able to give joyous thanks to the Father. Joy and patience are connected here. If we lose patience and gave
up the battle, how can we give joyous thanksgiving to
God for the victory? If we lose patience and fall into sin,
how can we have peace in our heart? If we do not have
patience with our brothers and sisters how can we
demonstrate the fruit of love? Patience is the soil in which
the Holy Spirit produces His fruit.

Wouldn't it be nice if we could become spiritually mature
overnight? The plants in our garden take time to grow.
Our young children mature over years. Maturity is a

process that takes time. It requires repentance, surrender, testing, sacrifice and obedience. Our faith is tested
and strengthened through the things we experience in
life. The work the Holy Spirit is doing in us will take a
lifetime. He will not stop working in us until we are in the
presence of the Father in heaven. If you want to become
all God wants you to become, you will need to be patient.
You will need to surrender to His work in your life. You
will need to endure testing and trials if you want to be
purified and matured.

PATIENCE AND THE PROMISES OF GOD

If you want to know victory, than patience is your greatest
friend. Very few battles are won without patience. Few
promises are fulfilled without the exercise of patience.
The writer of the book of Hebrews speaks about those
who inherited the promises of God through patience:

> We do not want you to become lazy, but to imitate
> those who through faith and patience inherit what
> has been promised. (Hebrews 6:12)

He said the same thing in Hebrews 10:36:

> You need to persevere so that when you have
> done the will of God, you will receive what he has
> promised.

Do you see the emphasis here? God is telling us that we
can only attain His promise by patience and perseverance. The reward is for those who have finished the race.
The crown is for those who have persevered to the end.
James illustrates this by using the example of a farmer
waiting for his crop:

> (5:7) Be patient, then, brothers, until the Lord's coming. See how the farmer waits for the land to yield its valuable crop and how patient he is for the autumn and spring rains. (5:8) You too, be patient and stand firm, because the Lord's coming is near. (James 5:7-8)

God has His timetable, which is not the same as ours. He is working out His purposes in a way that we do not understand. Just like the farmer has to wait for the seeds he sows to germinate, grow and produce fruit, so we too must learn to wait on the Lord. Blessing comes to those who wait.

Many times in my life I have sought the Lord for issues that burdened me greatly and did not see the result immediately. Imagine what would have happened had I given up after my first prayer? We have all read stories or heard testimonies of those who prayed and persevered and did not lose hope until they saw the Lord break through. Their patience was rewarded. Imagine the Old Testament prophets giving up after their first sermon. Imagine the evangelist never witnessing again because the first person he witnessed to laughed in his face. James tells us that we are to take as our example of patience the prophets of old.

> Brothers, as an example of patience in the face of suffering, take the prophets who spoke in the name of the Lord. (James 5:10)

These prophets of old preached when no one wanted to listen. Some didn't see any results for their preaching. Some, like Jeremiah, grieved over the call God had put on their lives. Others were persecuted. They were mocked, ridiculed, stoned and killed for their words, but they did not give up. They were patient to the very end. They held their position under tremendous stress and pressure. This, says James, is an example that we need to follow. God calls us to persevere. He asks us to be patient and to hold our position until He sends relief. Without patience it will be impossible to win that battle. Victory comes to the patient.

Isaiah tells us that we cannot even imagine the victory that God has in store for those who wait on God.

> Since ancient times no one has heard, no ear has perceived, no eye has seen any God besides you, who acts on behalf of those who wait for him. (Isaiah 64:4)

The victory is for those who wait patiently on the Lord. The apostle James reminds us of what God did for Job who patiently endured suffering in his day:

> As you know, we consider blessed those who have persevered. You have heard of Job's perseverance and have seen what the Lord finally brought about. The Lord is full of compassion and mercy. (James 5:11)

The Bible tells us that Job lost everything he had. His health was taken away. He lost the love and support of his wife. His family was killed. He was left in an ash heap with no pride left. He kept his eyes on the Lord and did not give up. His patience was rewarded when God finally broke through and blessed him. He would live in that wonderful blessing for the rest of his life.

Maybe you are facing a trial in your life today. Perhaps you have been feeling the strain of a difficult marriage. Maybe the Lord has taken away your health. Maybe your friends have abandoned you. Today you need the fruit of patience. You need the ability to bear the strain and pressure until there is a breaking through. This is the fruit of the Holy Spirit.

God wants to give you that fruit today. He wants to produce the fruit of patience in you so that you will be able to continue until all God's promises are fulfilled in you.

PATIENCE IS NECESSARY FOR CHARACTER TO BE BUILT IN US

Let me conclude with this final comment about patience. Paul reminds us in Romans 5:3-4 that character can only be built by patience in suffering:

> Not only so, but we also rejoice in our sufferings, because we know that suffering produces perseverance; perseverance, character; and character, hope.

Athletes know that if they do not stretch themselves in their ability to endure pressure and strain, they will never be able to compete. They push themselves in order to build up their muscles and endurance for the competition. It is the same in our walk with God. God is looking for people who will allow the Holy Spirit to produce this patience in them so that He can mature them in their faith. The patience Paul speaks about in Galatians 5:22 is not something that can be found in us naturally. The Holy Spirit gives us strength and endurance beyond our natural ability. He does this so that, as we remain under

that pressure long enough to be refined and matured into
the character of Jesus Christ.

For Consideration:

- How does God demonstrate patience toward us?
  How are we to show patience in our relationship
  with others?
- What is the connection between patience and the
  other fruit of the Holy Spirit? Can the fruit of the
  Holy Spirit be fully matured in us without patience?
- What does God promise will be the reward of patience in our lives?

For Prayer:

- Take a moment to thank the Lord for how He has
  been patient with you and your failures.
- Do you struggle to be patient with certain people
  in your life? Ask the Lord to help you to be more
  patient with them.
- Ask the Lord to help you to be patient under testing. Ask Him to teach you the lessons He wants
  you to learn in your trial?
- Thank the Lord for the blessing that result in the
  lives of those who are patient in suffering and trials.

CHAPTER 6

KINDNESS

The next fruit of the Spirit we will look at is the fruit of kindness. The word used for "kindness" in this passage can be translated by "moral excellence," "gentleness," or "goodness". It refers to an attitude of the heart that affects both speech and action.

As we begin our study of kindness, it is helpful to see the way the word and its roots are used in different contexts. We have an interesting use of the word in Romans 3:12 when Paul says:

> All have turned away, they have together become worthless; there is no one who does good, not even one.

The word that is translated as "good" in this verse is the same word used by Paul in Galatians 5:22 to describe the fruit of kindness. As God looked on the earth He saw that human beings had turned from Him and were no longer demonstrating kindness, gentleness or goodness. As Paul continues in this passage in Romans 3, he describes those who lacked this quality of goodness or kindness:

> (13) "Their throats are open graves; their tongues practice deceit." "The poison of vipers is on their lips." (14) "Their mouths are full of cursing and bitterness." (15) "Their feet are swift to shed blood; (16) ruin and misery mark their ways, (17) and the way of peace they do not know." (18) "There is no fear of God before their eyes." (Romans 3:13-18)

These verses are very important if we are to understand what Paul means in Galatians 3:22 about kindness as a fruit of the Spirit. The apostle describes for us here what it means to be without kindness. Notice two things he tells us about those who do not have the fruit of kindness (or goodness) in their lives.

First, those who lack of kindness demonstrate this in the way they speak. Notice how Paul describes the throats, tongues, lips and mouths of those who are without this fruit. Their throats are open graves, full of the smell of death and decay. Their language is foul and shows no respect. Their tongues speak deceit and they cannot be trusted. The poison of vipers is on their lips, hurting those who hear them. Their mouths are filled with cursing and bitterness.

Second, those who lack the quality of kindness demonstrate this in the way they live. In Romans 3:15-18 Paul describes these people as those whose feet are swift to shed blood. They do not pursue the way of peace. Everywhere they go they leave ruin and misery. There is little concern for the wellbeing of others in those who lack the fruit of kindness.

We have seen what Paul teaches about a lack of kindness. Let's take a moment now to consider what kindness is.

EASY BURDENS

The Greek word Paul uses for kindness in Galatians 5:22
comes from the word "*xrestos*" meaning easy, good,
gracious or kind. Jesus uses this root word in Matthew
11:30 when he says:

> For my yoke is easy and my burden is light.

The word "light" here is the word "*xrestos*" from which we
get the word kindness used by Paul in Galatians 5:22. In
this passage, Jesus is describing the burden He gives
those who belong to Him. He tells us that the burden He
gives us is "kind." It is not overwhelming or heavy to bear.
This helps us to understand what it means to be kind.

When you put a burden on a person that is too hard for
him or her to bear you are being unkind. We put burdens
on people by our words, actions and attitudes. Consider
what Paul said in Romans 3:12-18 about those who lack
the fruit of kindness. Their lips speak lies, bitterness and
anger. Has anyone ever lied to you? Has anyone ever
spoken to you in anger or bitterness? What does that do
to you? Does it not feel like they have given you a heavy
burden to bear? Sometimes the weight of those words is
so heavy we feel overwhelmed. What is true of words is
also true of how people react to us or the attitudes they
show toward us.

Those who show kindness will consider the effect of their
words, actions and attitudes on their brother or sister.

They will demonstrate compassion in what they say or do so that they are not burdening their brother or sister with a weight that is too heavy for them. God knows how much we can bear and give us what we can handle. He demonstrates perfect kindness in the burdens He gives.

As the Holy Spirit builds kindness in us, He will give us a greater awareness of the needs and burdens of those around us. Not only will He show us how we can refrain from burdening people with more than they can handle, but He will also show us how we can ease that burden to make it more bearable.

KINDNESS AND SACRIFICE

The greatest example of kindness can be seen in the character of God through Jesus Christ. Paul speaks of this in his epistle to the Ephesians.

> (2:6) And God raised us up with Christ and seated us with him in the heavenly realms in Christ Jesus, (2:7) in order that in the coming ages he might show the incomparable riches of his grace, expressed in his kindness to us in Christ Jesus. (Ephesians 2:6-7)

Notice how Paul speaks here about the expression of God's "kindness to us in Christ Jesus." This was demonstrated in the way He sent His son to die for us when we were still sinners. Imagine what God could have done to us as sinners? Instead, He showed tremendous kindness and compassion by sending His Son to die on our behalf. The kindness of Christ was seen in how he took our punishment on Himself and laid down His life as a sacrifice for our benefit.

Kindness demands a sacrifice. Kindness will deny itself in order to ease the burden of a brother or sister. The ultimate act of kindness is to lay down one's life as the Lord Jesus did for us. Not many of us will be required to make this ultimate sacrifice, but we will all be called on to make sacrifices of kindness for each other. These sacrifices will be sacrifices of our time, our effort or our resources. As the Holy Spirit produces the fruit of kindness in you, you will be more and more willing to put aside your own interests for the sake of those in need. You will be seeking ways of easing the burden of your brother or sister.

It is important that we note that the kindness of the Lord Jesus was demonstrated to those who rebelled against him. As the Holy Spirit produces kindness in us, we will not distinguish between friend and enemy. We will be kind to even those who hate us or do evil to us. Listen to what Jesus told his disciples in Luke 6:27-30:

> (6:27) "But I tell you who hear me: Love your enemies, do good to those who hate you, (6:28) bless those who curse you, pray for those who mistreat you. (6:29) If someone strikes you on one cheek, turn to him the other also. If someone takes your cloak, do not stop him from taking your tunic. (6:30) Give to everyone who asks you, and if anyone takes what belongs to you, do not demand it back.

Kindness reaches out to others unconditionally. It was when we were at our worst that the Lord reached out to us in kindness to save us.

> (3:3) At one time we too were foolish, disobedient, deceived and enslaved by all kinds of passions

and pleasures. We lived in malice and envy, being hated and hating one another. (3:4) But when the kindness and love of God our Savior appeared, (3:5) he saved us, not because of righteous things we had done, but because of his mercy. He saved us through the washing of rebirth and renewal by the Holy Spirit (Titus 3:3-5)

"When the kindness and love of God our Savior appeared, he saved us" (Titus 3:4). He did so by offering His life as the ultimate sacrifice for our sin. Kindness, as the fruit of the Spirit in our lives, will demand sacrifice. The kindness of the Lord Jesus in offering His life for ours is our model of perfect kindness. The Spirit of God produces this same attitude in those who belong to Christ.

KINDNESS AND FORGIVENESS

Paul tells us that kindness is also demonstrated in how we are willing to forgive those who have offended us.

> (3:12) Therefore, as God's chosen people, holy and dearly loved, clothe yourselves with compassion, kindness, humility, gentleness and patience. (3:13) Bear with each other and forgive whatever grievances you may have against one another. Forgive as the Lord forgave you (Colossians 3:12-13)

Not everyone is easy to get along with. Some people make our lives difficult. Paul told the Colossians that they were to bear with each other and forgive each other. In order to do this they needed to clothe themselves with compassion, kindness, humility, gentleness and patience.

Kindness is necessary if we are to forgive a brother or sister who has offended us.

Listen to what Paul told the Ephesians in Ephesians 4:32:

> Be kind and compassionate to one another, forgiving each other, just as in Christ God forgave you.

Notice again the connection between kindness and the ability to forgive a person who had offended. When a person sins against us, they can hurt us physically, emotionally or spiritually. Those who sin against us place themselves in our debt. Kindness is the ability to release a person from his or her debt to us.

How easy it is for us, when we have been hurt, to want the person who has hurt us to be reminded of what they have done. It is natural for us to want them to feel the weight of the harm they have caused us. Kindness removes that burden from the back of a brother or sister. It says: "I don't want you to be weighed down by the burden of what you have done to me. I want you to be free." This was the attitude the Holy Spirit wants to produce in us.

ENEMIES TO KINDNESS

In 1 Peter 2:1-3 the apostle speaks to his readers about the kindness (goodness) of the Lord and reminds them of their obligation now that they have seen this kindness (goodness):

> 2:1 Therefore, rid yourselves of all malice and all deceit, hypocrisy, envy, and slander of every kind.

2:2 Like newborn babies, crave pure spiritual milk, so that by it you may grow up in your salvation, 2:3 now that you have tasted that the Lord is good. (NIV)

When Peter says in 1 Peter 2:3 that his readers had "tasted that the Lord is good," he uses the same word Paul uses in Galatians 5:22 when he speaks of the fruit of kindness. In other words, those to whom Peter was writing had experienced the kindness of the Lord God toward them. Notice what Peter had to tell those who had tasted the kindness of the Lord. He told them to get rid of malice, deceit, hypocrisy, envy, and slander. If we want the Holy Spirit to produce the fruit of kindness in our lives, we must first let Him remove all these things from our heart. You cannot slander a brother and demonstrate kindness to him. Envy and jealousy are enemies to kindness. True kindness comes from a heart that is moved by the Spirit to seek the good of a brother or sister. It will sacrifice itself so that others might be blessed and their burden lifted. If you are not seeing kindness demonstrated in your life, then you need to examine your heart for evidence of envy and jealousy.

Is the fruit of kindness evident in your life? Take a moment to examine your words. Do they put a burden on others that is too heavy for them to bear? Examine your deeds. Do they show compassion toward both friends and enemies? Are you easing the burden your fellow human being is carrying? Examine your attitude. Is your attitude the same as Christ's toward those around you?

Kindness touches every aspect of our life. Kindness is expressed in actions, attitudes and speech. It is demonstrated in us because the Holy Spirit is living and producing the character of Christ in us. Kindness is very conscious of others and their needs. It is not self-centered. Kindness by nature is sacrificial. It longs to minister and ease the load its neighbor bears. It does this because it is driven by the heart of Christ to make the burden light and the yoke easy.

For Consideration:

- What is the connection between kindness and easing the burden of a brother or sister?
- Is kindness possible without some form of sacrifice?
- How is forgiveness an act of kindness? How is Christ's forgiveness a demonstration of His kindness toward us?
- What are the enemies of kindness?
- Gives some examples of how we can show kindness by the use of words.
- Give some examples of kindness in deeds.

For Prayer:

- Ask the Lord to open your eyes to the needs of others. Ask Him to make you more willing to respond to those needs in a kind manner.
- Thank the Lord for His great kindness toward you in offering His life on the cross for your sin.
- Are there people in your life you need to forgive? Ask God to give you grace to forgive them and release them from any burden they carry.
- Ask God to remove any enemies to kindness in your life.

- Ask God to help you to demonstrate kindness in word and deed. Ask Him to produce more kindness in you.

CHAPTER 7

GOODNESS

Goodness is the next fruit we will examine in this study. Goodness can be defined in terms of uprightness of heart and life. Something is seen as "good" if it is honorable or excellent in quality. Goodness is a very broad term. While goodness is a fruit of the Spirit, it produces fruit of its own. Evidence of goodness can be seen in a number of ways in the life of a believer. What is important to note is that goodness refers more to the character of an individual than to what that individual does. Many people can perform good deeds but they are not good in themselves.

THE LOSS OF GOODNESS

To understand the fruit of goodness we need to go back to the creation of mankind. After God created Adam and Eve, He looked over all He had created and saw that it was "good" (see Genesis 1:31). While human beings were created good, that goodness was destroyed with the entrance of sin into the world. The heart became evil. Genesis 6:5-6 describes what God saw when He looked at humankind in the days of Noah.

(5) The LORD saw how great man's wickedness
on the earth had become, and that every inclination of the thoughts of his heart was only evil all
the time. (6) The LORD was grieved that he had
made man on the earth, and his heart was filled
with pain.

Notice how evil had affected the heart of man. "Every
inclination of the thoughts of his heart was only evil all the
time" (Genesis 6:5-6). There was no goodness in the
thoughts of man according to this verse. All his thoughts
came from a heart that was stained by evil.

Writing to the Romans, Paul says:

(10) As it is written: "There is no one righteous,
not even one; (11) there is no one who understands, no one who seeks God. (12) All have
turned away, they have together become worthless; there is no one who does good, not even
one." (Romans 3:10-12)

There is very little room for goodness in this verse.
Consider what Paul says here:

1) There is no one righteous, not even one
2) There is no one who understands
3) No one seeks God
4) All have turned away
5) They have become worthless
6) There is no one who does good, not even one

While we may find this difficult to understand as human
beings, this is how God saw us. From the perspective of
holiness and purity, we were unclean. All our actions and

thoughts were stained by sin and unacceptable to a righteous God. There was no exception to this—not one person met God's standard for goodness. All had sinned and fell short of that standard (see Romans 3:23).

When it comes to goodness, God's definition is very different from ours. His standard is beyond us. His standard is perfection.

Imagine someone offering you a cup of poisoned water. Would you drink it? What if they squeezed some orange juice into the water to give it a better taste? Would you drink it then? No one in their right mind would drink from this cup. Sin is like poison in a cup. It affects everything we do. No matter what we do to our lives, until the poison of sin is removed, all our actions and thoughts will be an offense to a holy God.

True goodness is not possible until sin is addressed. This is why the Lord Jesus came. His work on the cross made goodness possible. The goodness Paul speaks about here is the fruit of the Spirit's work in our lives. It is not a natural goodness that comes from us, but goodness created and implanted into our lives by the Spirit of God.

GOOD FRUIT COMES FROM A GOOD HEART

Listen to what Jesus taught His disciples in Matthew 7:17-18:

> (7:17) Likewise every good tree bears good fruit, but a bad tree bears bad fruit. (7:18) A good tree cannot bear bad fruit, and a bad tree cannot bear good fruit.

Jesus teaches us that good fruit can only come from a good heart. If our heart is evil, then the fruit of that heart will be stained by evil as well. Only a pure heart can produce fruit that is acceptable to God—fruit that is good.

This same principle applies to the words we speak. Good words come from a good heart. Listen to what Jesus told the religious leaders of His day in Matthew 12:34-35:

> (12:34) You brood of vipers, how can you who are evil say anything good? For out of the overflow of the heart the mouth speaks. (12:35) The good man brings good things out of the good stored up in him, and the evil man brings evil things out of the evil stored up in him.

Notice that goodness refers to the quality of a heart that produces fruit. Goodness is only possible because of the work of the Lord Jesus on the cross to forgive sin and give us a new heart.

EXPRESSIONS OF GOODNESS IN THE BIBLE

Goodness is expressed in a variety of ways in Scripture. It is helpful to look at these expressions to get a better understanding of what its fruit looks like in the life of the believer.

Generosity

Goodness is expressed through acts of kindness and generosity. Jesus tells a story about a man who hired servants at different times in the day. Some servants were hired early in the morning and worked a full day. Others were hired later and only worked a few hours.

When it came time to pay the servants, the ones who had been working all day were surprised to find that they were not paid more than those who had served only a few hours. In response to their accusations of unfairness, the master responds:

> Don't I have the right to do what I want with my own money? Or are you envious because I am generous?' (Matthew 20:15)

The word translated "generous" in the New International Version is the word from which we get the word "goodness" used in Galatians 5:22. The master, in this case, was demonstrating goodness by being generous.

We see the same thought in the book of Acts. Here we read about Tabitha (also known as Dorcas) who was known for her acts of generosity and kindness as she ministered to the poor in her community. She is described in Acts 9:36 as having this quality of goodness.

> In Joppa there was a disciple named Tabitha (which, when translated, is Dorcas), who was always doing good and helping the poor.

We see here the connection between goodness and generosity. Goodness is demonstrated through acts of kindness and generosity.

Faithfulness

Another expression of goodness in the Scripture is faithfulness. Our Lord told a story about a master who left his possessions in the hands of his servants and went on a trip. When he returned he asked his servants to give an account of what they had done in his absence. One servant had doubled his master's resources. Listen to what the master told him in Matthew 25:21:

His master replied, "Well done, good and faithful servant! You have been faithful with a few things; I will put you in charge of many things. Come and share your master's happiness!"

The master called this servant "good" because he had been faithful with what he had given him.

The same thought is expressed in Luke 19:17:

'Well done, my good servant!' his master replied. 'Because you have been trustworthy in a very small matter, take charge of ten cities.'

The servant is called "good" because he had been trustworthy. As the Spirit of God produces the fruit of goodness in our lives it will be demonstrated by faithfulness to all God has called us to do.

Righteousness

There is also a connection in the Bible between "goodness" and righteousness. Joseph was a member of the Jewish Council. As a member of that Council he was a "good and upright man".

Now there was a man named Joseph, a member of the Council, a good and upright man (Luke 23:50)

Paul told Timothy that if a man cleansed himself, he could be useful to the Master for good work.

> If a man cleanses himself from the latter, he will be an instrument for noble purposes, made holy, useful to the Master and prepared to do any good work. (2 Timothy 2:21)

If we want to do good work for the Master the first thing that needs to happen is that we be cleansed of our impurity. Again this is the work of God's Spirit in our lives. He wants to cleanse us of our sin and impurities so that that our service for the Lord can be unhindered. As the Holy Spirit produces the fruit of goodness in our lives, He exposes and cleanses us of impure thoughts, actions and deeds.

Wholesome speech

Evidence of goodness will also be seen in how we speak. The apostle Paul wrote in Ephesians 4:29:

> Do not let any unwholesome talk come out of your mouths, but only what is helpful for building others up according to their needs, that it may benefit those who listen.

The word translated "helpful" in the New International Version is the word "good." Good speech is speech that builds up and encourages the body of Christ. Good speech is wholesome and healthy speech. If the Spirit is developing goodness in us, this will be reflected in how we speak to or about others.

TRUE GOODNESS IS OF GOD

True goodness comes from God and is the result of the ministry of the Holy Spirit in us. It is not the product of our own flesh. A man came to Jesus in Matthew 19 and asked Him what good thing he could do to inherit eternal life. Jesus told him, however, that there was only one person who was good.

> "Why do you ask me about what is good?" Jesus replied. "There is only One who is good. If you want to enter life, obey the commandments." (Matthew 19:17)

Jesus invited this man to follow the commandments, not as a means of obtaining eternal life but as a means of showing him that true and perfect goodness was impossible in human effort. According to Jesus, God alone was good. He was the measure of true goodness. To be good is to be like God. Not one of us can measure up to this standard.

While perfect goodness is impossible in the flesh, the Spirit of God continues to produce it in our lives. In Acts 11:24 Stephen is described as a good man. Notice the connection between his "goodness" and the filling of the Holy Spirit.

> He was a good man, full of the Holy Spirit and faith, and a great number of people were brought to the Lord.

Stephen's goodness was the direct result of the ministry of the Holy Spirit in his life producing the character of Christ in him.

The apostle John told his readers in 3 John 1:11 that those who do good are from God.

> Dear friend, do not imitate what is evil but what is good. Anyone who does what is good is from God. Anyone who does what is evil has not seen God.

The goodness Galatians 5:22 speaks about is the fruit of God's Spirit, making us more like God. It is not a natural goodness. All our "goodness" is stained by sin and unacceptable to God. What the Holy Spirit is producing in us is something different. It is the character of Christ being formed in us.

THERE IS NO SPIRITUAL GOOD IN US NATURALLY

Scripture makes it clear that there is no natural spiritual goodness in the flesh. You can see this tendency in a young child. As parents we always have to teach our children how to "be good." You never have to teach a child how to lie or hit his brother—that comes naturally. This is a reflection of the nature of the heart.

Paul tells us in Romans 7:18-19 that nothing good dwelt in his flesh.

> (7:18) I know that nothing good lives in me, that is, in my sinful nature. For I have the desire to do what is good, but I cannot carry it out. (7:19) For

what I do is not the good I want to do; no, the evil
I do not want to do--this I keep on doing.

What Paul tells us is very powerful. He makes it clear that
"nothing good" lived in his sinful nature. Jeremiah described the heart of man as being deceitful and beyond
cure:

> The heart is deceitful above all things and beyond
> cure. Who can understand it? (Jeremiah 17:9)

We may not feel this strongly about our heart and our
attitudes, but remember that God's standard is really
what counts here. It is not how we feel about ourselves
that matters but how God sees us. Scripture tells us that
God sees our hearts as evil and beyond cure.

GOD IS ABLE TO PRODUCE GOODNESS IN US

While goodness is not natural to our flesh, God is able to
produce goodness in us and equip us to do good works
in His name. Paul's prayer for the Corinthians was that
God reveal His grace in them so that they would have all
that was necessary to abound in good works.

> And God is able to make all grace abound to you,
> so that in all things at all times, having all that you
> need, you will abound in every good work. (2 Co-
> rinthians 9:8)

Notice here that it was necessary for God to make His
grace abound toward us so that we could be enabled to
abound in good works.

Paul's prayer for the Thessalonians was that the Lord God encourage and strengthen them in every good deed and word.

> (2:16) May our Lord Jesus Christ himself and God our Father, who loved us and by his grace gave us eternal encouragement and good hope, (2:17) encourage your hearts and strengthen you in every good deed and word. (2 Thessalonians 2:16-17)

The writer to the Hebrews prayed that God would equip his readers with everything good for doing His will.

> (13:20) May the God of peace, who through the blood of the eternal covenant brought back from the dead our Lord Jesus, that great Shepherd of the sheep, (13:21) equip you with everything good for doing His will, and may He work in us what is pleasing to Him, through Jesus Christ, to whom be glory for ever and ever. Amen. (Hebrews 13:20-21)

Paul told Timothy in 2 Timothy that God gave the Scripture so that His people could be thoroughly equipped for every good work.

> (3:16) All Scripture is God-breathed and is useful for teaching, rebuking, correcting and training in righteousness, (3:17) so that the man of God may be thoroughly equipped for every good work. (2 Timothy 3:16-17)

The point is clear. While we cannot produce true goodness in our sinful flesh, God alone is able to produce it in

us and equip us with all that is necessary to do good
work. The ability to do good that pleases God does not
come from the sinful heart and flesh but from the Spirit of
God who lives in us.

A CALL TO LIVE IN THE GOODNESS GOD GIVES

The call of Scripture to walk in goodness is very clear.
The Bible teaches that we have been created in Christ
Jesus to do good works. While good works do not save
us, they are the fruit of those who belong to the Lord
Jesus.

> For we are God's workmanship, created in Christ
> Jesus to do good works, which God prepared in
> advance for us to do. (Ephesians 2:10)

If we are to bear good fruit, we must surrender to the
work of God's Spirit in our lives.

The production of good fruit requires perseverance. Paul
tells us in Romans 2:7 that it is those who have persisted
in doing good who will inherit eternal life.

> To those who by persistence in doing good seek
> glory, honor and immortality, he will give eternal
> life.

Paul challenges us in Romans 12:9 to cling to what is
good.

> Love must be sincere. Hate what is evil; cling to
> what is good.

The Greek word used here for "cling" means to glue or to cement together. Paul tells us that we are to be securely fastened to the good the Holy Spirit is producing in us. The fact that we need to fasten ourselves firmly implies that the temptation to do the opposite is very real. While the Holy Spirit is producing the fruit of goodness in us, we must surrender to this work by persevering and clinging to what He is doing in us.

In Galatians, Paul reminds the believers that they were to do good to each other as often as they had opportunity. This required a conscious effort on their part.

> Therefore, as we have opportunity, let us do good to all people, especially to those who belong to the family of believers. (Galatians 6:10)

The Romans believers were challenged to overcome evil with good.

> Do not be overcome by evil, but overcome evil with good. (Romans 12:21)

We have been called and brought into the kingdom of God to demonstrate the fruit of goodness. We are to allow the Spirit of God to produce this work in us. As we surrender to Him, cling to what He is doing and respond in obedience, we bring praise and honor to the name of our God.

> In the same way, let your light shine before men, that they may see your good deeds and praise your Father in heaven. (Matthew 5:16)

Our good works testify to the presence of God in our lives because they are evidence of His fruit being produced in us.

The fruit of goodness demonstrates itself in kindness, generosity, wholesome words deeds and righteousness of heart. We must surrender to God if we are to demonstrate this fruit in our lives. The Lord promises to equip us in the production of good fruit but we must cling to Him and persevere in obedience. The extent to which goodness is produced in us may depend on how much we are willing to cooperate with God's Spirit who produces that goodness in us.

For Consideration:

- How does God see us in our natural condition?
- Can true goodness come from a heart that is stained by sin? While we can do good things in the flesh, why are those things not acceptable to God?
- What are some ways goodness is demonstrated in the life of the believer?
- What do we learn in this chapter about our need to cooperate with God in the production of the fruit of goodness in our lives?
- What evidence is there that the fruit of goodness is being produced in your life?

For Prayer:

- Thank the Lord that He did not abandon us in our sin.

- Thank the Lord that He wants to produce the fruit of goodness in us.
- Ask the Lord to show you how you can surrender more fully to Him as He produces the fruit of goodness in you.
- Ask God to enable you to persevere and be obedient to His leading as He produces a greater measure of the goodness of Christ in your life.

CHAPTER 8

FAITHFULNESS

When we think of faithfulness we usually think of the quality of someone who can stick with a task to the end. It often refers to someone who is reliable and dependable. There is a sense of this in the fruit we speak about here, but faithfulness goes deeper than this. The word "faithfulness" is the same word used in the New Testament for "faith." In fact, the translators of the King James Version use the word "faith" to speak of this fruit. What the Holy Spirit is producing in us here is faith.

FAITHFULNESS AS CONFIDENCE IN THE POWER OF GOD

The writer to the Hebrews defines faith in the following way:

> Now faith is being sure of what we hope for and certain of what we do not see. (Hebrews 11:1)

The person who is faithful (full of faith) is one who has a deep confidence in God and His Word. He knows with certainty that God will always do what He says.

There are many examples of this type of faith in the Scripture. In the Gospel of Matthew a centurion approached Jesus and asked Him to heal his young child. He knew that all Jesus had to do was to speak the word and his son would be healed, but he felt so unworthy that he did not believe he could even have Jesus enter his house. He reminded Jesus that, as a military commander, he would simply tell a soldier to do this or that and it would be done. He believed that all Jesus had to do was to speak to the sickness and tell it to go and the sickness would have to obey just as his soldiers did. When Jesus heard this, he told those present:

> "I tell you the truth, I have not found anyone in Israel with such great faith. (Matthew 8:10)

Faithfulness is demonstrated in the New Testament as a deep confidence and conviction in the power of God.

This was the conviction of the men who brought a paralytic friend to Jesus in Matthew 9:2.

> Some men brought to him a paralytic, lying on a mat. When Jesus saw their faith, he said to the paralytic, "Take heart, son; your sins are forgiven."

Notice that Jesus saw their faith as they brought their friend to Him. This faith was a deep conviction in their hearts that Jesus was able to heal their friend. They were full of faith in Jesus and His ability and willingness to heal. This stirred Jesus so that he reached out and touched their friend.

The one who is faithful has a deep conviction about God, His power and His sovereignty. This person places his or her confidence in the God of all power and might and trusts Him in all things. No matter how difficult things seem to be, the faithful person will keep looking to God because he or she knows that nothing is too difficult for Him. As the Holy Spirit works in our lives to produce faith, we will find ourselves having more and more confidence in God and His purposes.

FAITHFULNESS AS POWER

We have already seen that faithfulness has to do with our confidence in the power of God. When the men brought their paralytic friend to Jesus in Matthew 9, Jesus noticed their faith and responded. Faith released the power of God. We see this often in Scripture.

On one occasion some blind men were brought to Jesus to be healed. Notice what Jesus said to these men in Matthew 9:29:

> Then he touched their eyes and said, "According to your faith will it be done to you" (Matthew 9:29)

These blind men would be healed according to their faith. We understand from this that faith was an important ingredient in their healing.

In the book of Acts, Paul met a man who was crippled in his feet. When Paul looked at this cripple, God revealed to him that he had faith to be healed.

> (14:9) He listened to Paul as he was speaking. Paul looked directly at him, saw that he had faith

> to be healed (14:10) and called out, "Stand up on
> your feet!" At that, the man jumped up and began
> to walk. (Acts 14:9-10)

It was when Paul saw that the cripple had faith to be
healed that he told him to stand up. The man was healed
as a result of this faith in God.

Notice the connection between faith and ministry in 2
Corinthians 10:15. Writing to the Corinthians Paul said:

> Neither do we go beyond our limits by boasting of
> work done by others. Our hope is that, as your
> faith continues to grow, our area of activity among
> you will greatly expand.

We can't miss what Paul is saying here. He told them that
as their faith grew, the apostle's activity among them
would greatly expand. Their faith would release the
power of God in a fresh way and expand His kingdom in
their midst.

What we understand from these passages is that faith is
the soil in which the power of God is demonstrated.
Where there is no faith, there is very little evidence of
God's power. As our faith grows, so does God's work in
and through us.

FAITHFULNESS AS A CONVICTION OF THE TRUTH OF GOD

As the apostles moved from region to region, they spread
the teaching about Jesus and His work. This word
spread, and a great number of people believed. Acts 6:7
tells us that many priests became obedient to the faith.

So the word of God spread. The number of disciples in Jerusalem increased rapidly, and a large number of priests became obedient to the faith.

The use of the word faith here has more to do with the teaching of God's Word than demonstrations of power. The same use of the word can be seen in Acts 14:21-22:

> (14:21) They preached the good news in that city and won a large number of disciples. Then they returned to Lystra, Iconium and Antioch, (14:22) strengthening the disciples and encouraging them to remain true to the faith. "We must go through many hardships to enter the kingdom of God," they said.

Again we see the connection between the preaching of the good news in verse 21 and encouraging the disciples to remain strong in the faith in verse 22. In other words, remaining in the faith had to do with continuing to believe the truths that were handed down by the apostles.

In 2 Corinthians 13:5 Paul challenged the Corinthians to test themselves to see if they were still in the faith.

> Examine yourselves to see whether you are in the faith; test yourselves. Do you not realize that Christ Jesus is in you--unless, of course, you fail the test?

How were the Corinthians to examine themselves here? The context of 2 Corinthians 13 relates to those who wondered if what Paul spoke was really from God (see 2 Corinthians 13:3). It is in this context that Paul challenges the Corinthians to test themselves. What he is asking them to do is to examine their hearts to see whether what they believed and what he taught lined up with the truth of the Word of God.

To be in the faith is to be true to Scripture. He who is faithful is true to the Word of God. A faithful person loves and obeys the Word of God. As the Spirit of God produces faithfulness in us, we will find an increasing desire for the Word of God and a deeper conviction of the truth of that Word.

FAITHFULNESS AS PERSEVERANCE

There are many verses in the New Testament that speak about faith and perseverance. Those who are faithful persevere, despite the obstacles or difficulties placed on their path.

Paul reminds Timothy that there were some among him that had listened to false and opposing ideas and had turned away from the faith.

> (6:20) Timothy, guard what has been entrusted to your care. Turn away from godless chatter and the opposing ideas of what is falsely called knowledge, (6:2) which some have professed and in so doing have wandered from the faith. (1 Timothy 6:20-21)

These individuals wandered from the faith because they had not persevered in the truth that had been taught them.

Speaking to Timothy again in 2 Timothy 2:17-18, Paul warned him about the false prophets and teachers in their midst:

> 2:17 Their teaching will spread like gangrene. Among them are Hymenaeus and Philetus, 2:18 who have wandered away from the truth. They say that the resurrection has already taken place, and they destroy the faith of some.

Notice that there were individuals who believed this false teaching and wandered from the faith. They did not persevere in truth but fell into false teaching.

Jude challenged his readers to contend for the faith. In other words, they were to fight to keep the purity of the truth that had been passed down to them.

> Dear friends, although I was very eager to write to you about the salvation we share, I felt I had to write and urge you to contend for the faith that was once for all entrusted to the saints. (Jude 1:3)

The enemy seeks to turn many from the truth of God's Word. The faithful person will not fall into his trap. He will stand firm in this truth. He will fight for the truth of the Word of God. The enemy would like nothing more than to destroy the faith of God's people. When Paul wrote to the Thessalonians he was afraid that the tempter had already taken them away from their faith.

> For this reason, when I could stand it no longer, I sent to find out about your faith. I was afraid that in some way the tempter might have tempted you

and our efforts might have been useless. (1 Thessalonians 3:5)

We are in the midst of a battle for faith. Paul understood that Satan would attack those who belonged to Christ and walked in His truth.

As Jesus prepared to return to His father, he prayed particularly for the faith of Peter in Luke 22:32:

> But I have prayed for you, Simon, that your faith may not fail. And when you have turned back, strengthen your brothers.

Satan would do all he could to destroy Peter's faith. Jesus prayed that his faith would not fail. That is to say, that Peter would continue to remain faithful to the truth He had learned and walk in it despite the efforts of the enemy to sidetrack him.

The faithful person will stand firm in his faith despite the obstacles that come his or her way. He will hold his ground and not give in to the enemy. Paul reminds Timothy that he was in the midst of a spiritual battle for faith. He challenges him to be faithful in that battle.

> Fight the good fight of the faith. Take hold of the eternal life to which you were called when you made your good confession in the presence of many witnesses. (1 Timothy 6:12)

As Paul looked back on his life, he rejoiced at the fruit of faithfulness the Spirit of God had produced in him. Though there were many temptations, he had fought a good fight and had kept the faith.

> I have fought the good fight, I have finished the race, I have kept the faith. (2 Timothy 4:7)

The writer to the Hebrews was confident that his readers would demonstrate the fruit of faith in their battle against the enemy. Though the pressure mounted they would not shrink back.

> But my righteous one will live by faith. And if he shrinks back, I will not be pleased with him." But we are not of those who shrink back and are destroyed, but of those who believe and are saved. (Hebrews 10:38-39)

The person who is faithful will "live by faith' and not shrink back. He will persevere though the pressure mounts. He will remain true to the Word and faithful to his God. The faithfulness the Holy Spirit is creating in us is the ability to remain strong in the face of obstacles and trials.

THE ENEMIES TO FAITHFULNESS

There are many enemies to faithfulness in Scripture. Let's take a moment to examine some of these enemies.

Error and False Teaching

As we have already seen, faithfulness has to do with holding onto the truth of God's Word. A faithful person remains true to the truth of the Word of God. The enemy has watered down the truth of God's Word and caused others to turn from it. Many have fallen into this error.

> (6:20) Timothy, guard what has been entrusted to your care. Turn away from godless chatter and

the opposing ideas of what is falsely called knowledge, (6:21) which some have professed and in so doing have wandered from the faith. (1 Timothy 6:20-21)

Error and false teaching are enemies to faith. You cannot be faithful if you turn from the truth of the Word of God. The faithful person is one who is absolutely committed to the teaching of the Scripture.

Money

Paul reminds Timothy of the dangers of money and how it had caused many to wander from the faith.

For the love of money is a root of all kinds of evil. Some people, eager for money, have wandered from the faith and pierced themselves with many griefs. (1 Timothy 6:10)

Money and worldly possessions are a second enemy to faithfulness. Many have turned from the faith because they have loved the things of this world too much. You cannot be faithful if your heart is divided.

Fear

Jesus rebuked His disciples in Mark 4:40 because they had allowed their fear to steal away their faith.

He said to his disciples, "Why are you so afraid? Do you still have no faith?"

While fear is often a natural response to a trying situation, it will not paralyze those who have faith. Where fear controls, however, faith is lost.

Doubt

Doubt is also an enemy to faith. The faithful person is one who has cast off doubt. You cannot be a doubter and faithful at the same time.

> But when he asks, he must believe and not doubt, because he who doubts is like a wave of the sea, blown and tossed by the wind. (James 1:6)

Faith relates to confidence in God. The faithful person is one who trusts the Word of the Lord and will stand firmly on that Word.

Disobedience

Disobedience is another enemy of faith. A faithful person is one who walks in obedience to the Word of God. Abraham is described as faithful because he was obedient to the Lord.

> By faith Abraham, when called to go to a place he would later receive as his inheritance, obeyed and went, even though he did not know where he was going. (Hebrews 11:8)

You can't be faithful if you are not obedient. God does not force us to obey. We have a choice to make. We can be faithful or we can be disobedient but we cannot be both.

Inactivity

James has much to say about faith in his epistle. One principle that comes through very powerfully in the Epistle of James is that inactivity is a great enemy of faith. Listen to what James has to say about this:

> What good is it, my brothers, if a man claims to have faith but has no deeds? Can such faith save him? ... As the body without the spirit is dead, so faith without deeds is dead. (James 2:14; 26)

James is telling us that if we say we have faith we must do something about it. A faithful person is an active person. His faith moves him to do something. He is not content to see a need and not do something about it. His faith and his works walk hand in hand. Inactivity is the natural enemy of faith. He who says he has faith but does nothing about it is unfaithful.

GROWING IN FAITHFULNESS

Scripture challenges us to cooperate with the Holy Spirit as He produces the fruit of faithfulness in our lives. There are a number of ways we can do this.

Fellowship with other believers

Acts 11 tells us of how Barnabas arrived in the church in Antioch and encouraged them in their faith. The presence of Barnabas, who had come all the way from Jerusalem to see what God was doing, blessed the church in Antioch and his fellowship with the church in Antioch strengthened their faith.

> When he arrived and saw the evidence of the grace of God, he was glad and encouraged them all to remain true to the Lord with all their hearts. (Acts 11:23)

Paul sent Timothy to Thessalonica to strengthen the faith of the believers in the church.

> We sent Timothy, who is our brother and God's fellow worker in spreading the gospel of Christ, to strengthen and encourage you in your faith (1 Thessalonians 3:2)

Paul prayed that God would give him the opportunity to be with the Thessalonians so that he could strengthen them in their faith.

> Night and day we pray most earnestly that we may see you again and supply what is lacking in your faith. (1 Thessalonians 3:10)

Writing to the Romans Paul said:

> (1:11) I long to see you so that I may impart to you some spiritual gift to make you strong—(1:12) that is, that you and I may be mutually encouraged by each other's faith. (Romans1:11-12)

Faith is strengthened in fellowship with other believers. As believers, we minister and encourage each other in our walk of faith. A believer who wants to grow in the fruit of faithfulness will seek out other believers.

Hearing the Word

Faith is strengthened by the Word of God.

> Consequently, faith comes from hearing the mes-
> sage, and the message is heard through the word
> of Christ. (Romans 10:17)

The Word of God strengthens faith. It encourages our
faith and trust in God. Its examples demonstrate faith in
the lives of the men and women who have gone before
us. The Holy Spirit will use the Word of God to build up
our faith.

Paul told Timothy that the goal of instruction in the Word
of God was love from a sincere faith.

> The goal of this command is love, which comes
> from a pure heart and a good conscience and a
> sincere faith. (1 Timothy 1:5)

We teach God's word not just for knowledge. The goal of
teaching God's Word ought to be to stir up love and
sincere faith.

Reproof

Paul encouraged Titus to rebuke those who were teaching false doctrine so they would have a sound faith.

> This testimony is true. Therefore, rebuke them
> sharply, so that they will be sound in the faith (Ti-
> tus 1:13)

If you want to grow in faith you will need to learn how to accept the reproof of your brothers and sisters in Christ. Often the Holy Spirit will use our brothers or sisters to challenge us or bring us back to the path of faith.

CONCLUDING COMMENTS

Faithfulness will keep us from the enemy

Faith is required if we are to be protected from the enemy. Paul speaks of faith as our shield in Ephesians 6:16. In 1 Thessalonians 5:8 he speaks of it as our breastplate. These are necessary pieces of armor if we want to be protected from the enemy and his attacks.

Peter tells us that we are shielded by our faith and kept by God.

> ... who through faith are shielded by God's power until the coming of the salvation that is ready to be revealed in the last time. (1 Peter 1:5)

Faith is our protection from the attacks of the enemy. The Holy Spirit produces the fruit of faith in us so that we can withstand these attacks.

Faith is our victory

Not only is faith our protection from the enemy, it is also our guarantee of victory.

> ... for everyone born of God overcomes the world. This is the victory that has overcome the world, even our faith. (1 John 5:4)

To resist and overcome the devil we must do so by faith.

> Resist him, standing firm in the faith, because you
> know that your brothers throughout the world are
> undergoing the same kind of sufferings. (1 Peter
> 5:9)

To resist is to hold our ground. The enemy wants to take everything he can from us but we must resist him and keep what has been entrusted to us by the Holy Spirit. We do this by standing firm in the truth that has been revealed to us. As we stand firm, the enemy has no foothold in our life. He is defeated by our faithfulness to God and His Word.

Without faith we cannot please God

Hebrews 11:6 makes it quite clear that if we want to please God, we must have faith. We must believe Him and trust in His purposes.

> And without faith it is impossible to please God,
> because anyone who comes to him must believe
> that he exists and that he rewards those who ear-
> nestly seek him.

We cannot honor God if we do not have faith. It is the purpose of the Holy Spirit to produce this faith in us. He wants us to come to a place of absolute confidence and obedience to the Lord. He wants us to overcome the temptations of the enemy. To do this, He works in us producing the fruit of faith. Once again, this is not something natural to our flesh but a wonderful work of the Spirit of God in our lives. Let us surrender to this work though it may bring us into deep trial and trouble for it is the path to victory and greater maturity in Christ.

For Consideration:

- Have you been growing in your confidence and trust in God and His purposes?
- What evidence is there of a God's power in your life?
- What is the connection between faithfulness and our conviction of the truth of His Word? Can we be faithful if we are not walking in the truth of God's Word?
- How does faith strengthen us in the trials of life?
- What are the enemies of faith? Have you been struggling personally with any of these enemies?
- What do we learn in this chapter about how to grow in faith?

For Prayer:

- Ask God to help you to have a greater confidence in His Word and in His promises.
- Ask God to give you a faith that will allow His power to be more active in your life. Ask Him to give you a faithfulness that allows greater fruit to be produced in your life and ministry.
- Are you facing a trial in your life today? Ask God to strengthen your faith so you can overcome. Ask Him to protect you so that your faith will remain strong.
- What are your personal enemies to faith? Ask God to give you victory over these enemies.

CHAPTER 9

GENTLENESS

Gentleness is defined as meekness, humility and consideration of others. It also relates to our willingness to accept the circumstances the Lord sends our way. The word gentleness is not often used in Scripture. We can, however, get a sense of its meaning by examining how it is used by New Testament writers. It is also helpful to consider some examples of those who demonstrated gentleness in their lives. We will examine this fruit of the Spirit from both of these perspectives.

GENTLENESS IN THE MIDST OF OPPOSITION

As we begin our study of gentleness we need to see how it affects our relationship with other people. Listen to what Paul tells Timothy in 2 Timothy 2:25 about the servant of God:

> Those who oppose him he must gently instruct, in the hope that God will grant them repentance leading them to a knowledge of the truth

Paul gives an example of a Christian worker who was being opposed by someone under his authority. He was to be gentle with those who opposed him. He was to "gently instruct" them in the hope that God would grant them repentance.

What is our natural tendency when we are opposed? We tend to speak harshly and critically to those who oppose us. Gentleness, however, does not act harshly. It speaks with kindness and consideration, even to our enemies.

Jesus' teaching was to turn the other cheek when we are opposed.

> But I tell you, do not resist an evil person. If someone strikes you on the right cheek, turn to him the other also. (Matthew 5:39)

It is not easy to turn the other cheek. Jesus is not telling us here that we should invite opposition. What He is telling us, however, is that when opposed we are not to seek revenge. We are to accept opposition, trusting God to reveal His purpose. To be gentle is to demonstrate great patience with those who oppose us. Gentleness responds with humility and meekness.

Isaiah prophesied that the Messiah would demonstrate this spirit of gentleness. Listen to what he said in Isaiah 53:7:

> He was oppressed and afflicted, yet he did not open his mouth; he was led like a lamb to the slaughter, and as a sheep before her shearers is silent, so he did not open his mouth.

Jesus did not retaliate or seek to defend Himself against those who opposed Him. He silently and meekly accepted the purpose of God for His life.

The Holy Spirit desires to produce gentleness in our lives. This gentleness responds with meekness and humility to difficult circumstances in life. It does not seek revenge but commits all matters to the Lord.

GENTLENESS IN RELATIONSHIPS

In Titus 3:1 the apostle Paul challenged Titus to remind those under him to show consideration to all men.

> (3:1) Remind the people to be subject to rulers and authorities, to be obedient, to be ready to do whatever is good, (3:2) to slander no one, to be peaceable and considerate, and to show true humility toward all men.

The word "considerate" comes from the same word Paul uses in Galatians 5:23 to speak of gentleness. Gentleness, in this context, has to do with being considerate. Paul explains what he means by being considerate to the Philippians when he told them:

> (2:3) Do nothing out of selfish ambition or vain conceit, but in humility consider others better than yourselves. 2:4 Each of you should look not only to your own interests, but also to the interests of others. (Philippians 2:3-4)

To be considerate is to consider the needs of others as being more important than our own. It is to look to the needs and interests of another person and not place ourselves first. Paul continued in Philippians 2 to give the Philippians the example of the Lord Jesus and His attitude.

> (2:5) Your attitude should be the same as that of Christ Jesus: (2:6) Who, being in very nature God, did not consider equality with God something to be grasped, (2:7) but made himself nothing, taking the very nature of a servant, being made in human likeness. (2:8) And being found in appearance as a man, he humbled himself and became obedient to death-- even death on a cross! (Philippians 2:5-8)

The Lord Jesus demonstrated gentleness by humbling Himself and becoming a man. He also showed humility and gentleness by serving and giving His life for mankind. Gentleness considers the needs of others before its own needs.

The New Testament urges us to be gentle in our dealings with others.

> Be completely humble and gentle; be patient, bearing with one another in love. (Ephesians 4:2)

Notice that gentleness is connected with patience and bearing with a brother or sister in love. This same connection is seen in Colossians 3:12-13:

> (3:12) Therefore, as God's chosen people, holy and dearly loved, clothe yourselves with compassion, kindness, humility, gentleness and patience. (3:13) Bear with each other and forgive whatever

grievances you may have against one another. Forgive as the Lord forgave you.

Gentleness requires being patience with each other. This is not always easy. Sometimes people seem to get on our nerves and irritate us. The gentle person is able to look beyond those irritations, considering the interests of those who are difficult to love as well as those who are easy to love. He bears with the weaknesses of a brother or sister. He forgives when a brother or sister offends. He shows kindness and respect when opposed. He does this because this is the heart of Christ toward him.

Paul told the Galatian churches to restore a brother caught in sin with gentleness.

> Brothers, if someone is caught in a sin, you who are spiritual should restore him gently. But watch yourself, or you also may be tempted. (Galatians 6:1)

We need this reminder. Gentleness is a necessary ingredient in any church discipline. How easy it is in the heat of the moment to lose sight of gentleness. How easy it is to look down on those who have fallen into sin. The goal of discipline is restoration. When gentleness is missing in discipline, we often do more damage than good. Gentleness will consider the brother and his pain at the moment. It will not excuse sin but it will treat the sinner with respect.

To be gentle is to be understanding and accepting. It is not harsh or critical. As the Holy Spirit works in us to produce gentleness we will find ourselves more willing to consider the needs of a brother or sister in Christ. Our pride and self-centeredness will be rebuked and we will be called on to be more compassionate and considerate of even those who are difficult to love.

GENTLENESS IN REBUKE

True gentleness is also seen in how we receive rebuke or discipline. Listen to what James tells us in James 1:21:

> Therefore, get rid of all moral filth and the evil that is so prevalent and humbly accept the word planted in you, which can save you.

The word "humbly" comes from the same root word Paul uses for gentleness. In other words, we are to receive the word with gentleness. The context of this verse relates to dealing with sin in our life. When we are living in sin and confronted by the Word of God, we are to receive rebuke with gentleness. We are to humbly surrender to what God is telling us.

To be gentle is to be humble enough to admit we are wrong. To be gentle is to be willing to confess that we need to change. It is to place ourselves before the Lord and to let Him do whatever He needs to do in our life to change any offensive attitude or action.

How important this fruit is in the life of the church. We have all met leaders who are unwilling to admit they are wrong. We have met believers who persist in sin because they do not want to look bad before others. True gentleness will surrender to the Word of God. It will admit its wrongdoings and confess them before God. The gentle person accepts reproof and rebuke and is better for it.

GENTLENESS IN MINISTRY

James tells us that we are to live our lives before others in a way that demonstrates gentleness that comes from wisdom.

> Who is wise and understanding among you? Let him show it by his good life, by deeds done in the humility that comes from wisdom. (James 1:13)

Notice the word humility in James 1:13. Again the word comes from the same root as the word "gentleness" in Galatians 5:23. What James is telling us here is that we are to live a good life that demonstrates deeds done in humility (gentleness) and wisdom.

We demonstrate the character of Christ through the gentleness of our deeds. This is seen in our relationships with others. It is seen in how we accept rebuke and correction. It is seen in our response to opposition and in considering the needs of others as more important than our own. As we minister in the name of the Lord we are to do so with gentleness.

Gentleness is not only to be seen in our deeds but also in our words. The apostle Peter challenged believers to ready at all times to give an answer for the hope they had.

> But in your hearts set apart Christ as Lord. Always be prepared to give an answer to everyone who asks you to give the reason for the hope that you have. But do this with gentleness and respect (1 Peter 3:15)

Notice that Peter told his readers that they were to answer with gentleness and respect. How easy it is to be critical and condemning when challenged in what we believe. Maybe you have sat under the preaching of a pastor who lacked this gentleness. Gentleness does not mean that we compromise truth or refrain from speaking about sin in our midst. The gentle person, however, speaks with compassion and love. He does not speak in pride, but realizes that were it not for the protecting hand of God, he too could have fallen into the same sin. Gentleness speaks with humility and deep concern. It does not look down on an individual who has fallen. It does not speak rudely to the person who does not believe the same things he does. Speaking with gentleness is evidence of the Holy Spirit in our lives.

This gentleness is not natural to our flesh. We are self-centered by nature. When rebuked, we often react selfishly. When opposed we push our way through, ignoring the advice of others. Many problems in the church of our day could be avoided if we would only let the Holy Spirit produce in us a greater measure of gentleness.

As the Holy Spirit produces gentleness in us, pride and selfishness are exposed. The harsh and critical spirit is removed. Our eyes are opened to see others in a new way. We find ourselves more willing to accept the trials that come our way to strengthen our faith. We submit with humbleness to the will and purpose of God even when it hurts. We receive with thanksgiving the godly rebuke of concerned brothers and sisters challenging us to greater maturity. Gentleness creates a humble and submissive spirit in which God is free to work.

For Consideration:

- What is the response of a gentle person to opposition?
- How does the fruit of gentleness affect how we see others?
- How does the gentle person respond to rebuke?
- In what way does gentleness open doors to more effective ministry to the people around us?
- What problems are caused in the church today by of a lack of gentleness?
- How has the Lord Jesus been gentle to you?

For Prayer:

- Ask God to give you more gentleness in your relationships with those around you.
- Have you shown a lack of gentleness in receiving rebuke or correction? Ask the Lord to humble you so you can receive rebuke and correction.
- Ask God to give you more grace to accept the circumstances He brings into your life.
- Has there been a lack of gentleness in dealing with sin and disagreements among believers in your fellowship? Ask the Spirit of God to produce more gentleness among believers in your fellowship group.
- Take a moment to thank the Lord for His incredible gentleness in your life.

CHAPTER 10

SELF-CONTROL

The last fruit we will examine is the fruit of self-control. The term self-control may be to some extent misleading. When we speak of self-control we generally understand it to be the ability to master one's actions, passions, desires and emotions. Even the unbeliever is able to demonstrate self-control. Remember, however, that we are speaking here not about a natural ability but a fruit of the Spirit. In other words, the self-control we are speaking about is the direct result of the work of the Holy Spirit in our lives.

It is the desire of the Holy Spirit to enable us to control of our actions, passions, emotions, and desires so that we are more like Christ. This is only possible as we surrender to His ministry and leading. There is an element of human will in our surrender but we also know that without the work of the Spirit to change our human will, our battle with sin, passions and desires would often be futile. The pull of the flesh is very powerful. When insulted or angered, the flesh wants to lash out. When tempted, it wants to yield. How does the believer overcome these fleshly impulses? This is the ministry of the Holy Spirit in us. It is His desire to strengthen us to overcome. He enables us to resist and walk in obedience to the Word of God.

While we must co-operate with the Holy Spirit in this matter, this fruit has its origin in God and not in man. Throughout the history of the church many have exercised a self-control that is human in nature. They have disciplined themselves, isolated themselves and done all manner of things to themselves in an attempt to get closer to God. Their efforts, though admirable, were fleshly in nature.

There is a radical difference, between self-control that has its origins in human effort and self-control that is the fruit of the Holy Spirit in us. When self-control is the result of the ministry of the Holy Spirit, there is power and perseverance. We exercise this self-control because we are being moved and motivated not by the flesh but by the Holy Spirit who is shaping us into the image of Christ.

EXAMPLES OF SELF-CONTROL

David

In 1 Samuel 24 Saul was resting in the front of a cave where David and his men were hiding. For David's men, this was a God-given opportunity to kill Saul and finally be set free from this lifestyle of hiding and fleeing.

> (24:4) The men said, "This is the day the LORD spoke of when he said to you, `I will give your enemy into your hands for you to deal with as you wish.'" Then David crept up unnoticed and cut off a corner of Saul's robe. (24:5) Afterward, David

> was conscience-stricken for having cut off a cor-
> ner of his robe. (24:6) He said to his men, "The
> LORD forbid that I should do such a thing to my
> master, the LORD's anointed, or lift my hand
> against him; for he is the anointed of the LORD."
> (24:7) With these words David rebuked his men
> and did not allow them to attack Saul. And Saul
> left the cave and went his way. (1 Samuel 24:4-7)

This was the opportunity David's men had been looking
for. Saul had been seeking David's life and wanted to kill
him. Now David had the opportunity to rid himself of this
terrible threat. The death of Saul would have meant his
personal freedom as well as that of his men.

As David crept silently toward Saul, you can almost hear
the voice of the Spirit calling out to David not to harm the
anointed one of the Lord. David had a decision to make.
Would he listen to the voice of the Spirit or would he
listen to his flesh? David surrendered to the inner voice of
the Spirit.

The Disciples

In the Gospel of Luke, Jesus was traveling to Jerusalem.
As He traveled, He sent word ahead that He was passing
through the region of Samaria. When the Samaritans
heard that Jesus was going to Jerusalem, they refused to
welcome Him because of their hatred for the city. This
angered James and John. Listen to their response:

> When the disciples James and John saw this,
> they asked, "Lord, do you want us to call fire
> down from heaven to destroy them?" 9:55 But Je-
> sus turned and rebuked them (Luke 9:54-55)

James and John listened to their flesh. They wanted to call down fire from heaven to destroy the Samaritans who had rejected the Lord Jesus. The voice of the flesh is sometimes very powerful. How often have we found ourselves in a similar situation? We hear something that angers us and the flesh begins to cry out for revenge. In an instant, we explode in anger and speak words we later regret. This is the situation James and John found themselves in.

Notice, however, that Jesus rebuked them and their attitude. In a similar way, the Spirit of God rebukes our angry or fleshly attitude. He reminds us of the purpose of God and the teaching of His Word. The Spirit of God restrains us and convicts us, protecting us from the flesh and its evil desires. He is producing the fruit of self-control in us.

The Athlete

Paul speaks of self-control in the life of the athlete in 1 Corinthians 9:25-27:

> (9:25) Everyone who competes in the games goes into strict training. They do it to get a crown that will not last; but we do it to get a crown that will last forever. (9:26) Therefore I do not run like a man running aimlessly; I do not fight like a man beating the air. (9:27) No, I beat my body and make it my slave so that after I have preached to others, I myself will not be disqualified for the prize.

The apostle told his listeners that, in his life and ministry, he disciplined himself and held his body in subjection to the greater purposes of God. As the athlete runs in the race, his lungs burn and his heart pounds with the strain. His feet hurt and his legs ache. He knows, however, that if he listens to his body he will lose the race. Instead of listening at what his body is saying, he looks ahead to the prize before him. He listens to the call of the prize and not the cry of his body. Paul kept his eyes fixed on Jesus as the prize, and depended on the strength and leading of His Spirit. He demonstrated the fruit of self-control by holding his body in subjection to the purposes and leading of the Holy Spirit. He drew on the strength the Spirit of God provided to keep on even when naturally he would have wanted to give up.

These examples show us the role of the Spirit in producing the fruit of self-control in our lives. He rebukes, restrains, disciplines and strengthens the believer, enabling him or her to resist the impulses of the flesh to live as God requires.

TEACHING OF SCRIPTURE REGARDING SELF-CONTROL

Having looked at these examples, let's take a moment now to examine some further teaching of Scripture about self-control in the life of the believer.

Required for an elder

Paul tells us that an elder must be self-controlled.

> Rather he must be hospitable, one who loves what is good, who is self-controlled, upright, holy and disciplined. (Titus 1:8)

Anyone who seeks a position of leadership in the church of Jesus Christ must be willing to die to the flesh and surrender to the teaching of Scripture and the leading of the Spirit of God. They must seek the strength of the Holy Spirit for victory over the lusts of their flesh. They must walk in obedience to the Word of God and the conviction of the Spirit of God in their life.

Self-Control and Knowledge

Peter reminds us that as believers we are to make every effort to add self-control to our knowledge of God and His Word.

> (1:5) For this very reason, make every effort to add to your faith goodness; and to goodness, knowledge; (1:6) and to knowledge, self-control; and to self-control, perseverance; and to perseverance, godliness (2 Peter 1:5-6)

It is one thing to have the knowledge of God and His purpose, but it is another to have self-control. You can have a Bible College or Seminary training and know all there is to know about God's character and plan, but if you do have the ability to live in that truth, it does you no good. People not only want to understand the truth, they also want to see that truth demonstrated in the lives of those who claim it. Self-control and knowledge must walk hand in hand. He who claims to know that truth must demonstrate it in word and deed. This is the work of the Holy Spirit in us who not only teaches us the truth of the Word of God but enables us to apply that truth to our lives by convicting and disciplining us in godly living.

Self-control and Righteousness

In Acts 24:25 Paul spoke to Felix about righteousness, self-control and the judgment to come.

> As Paul discoursed on righteousness, self-control and the judgment to come, Felix was afraid and said, "That's enough for now! You may leave. When I find it convenient, I will send for you." (NIV)

Self-control and righteousness are very closely tied. There will be, throughout our lives, an ongoing battle with sin and the flesh. We cannot live the life God requires unless we die to the impulses of the flesh. The fruit of self-control is the Spirit-given ability to resist the impulses of the flesh walk in the righteous purpose of God.

Turning the Other Cheek

Self-control in the Christian life is demonstrated in how we respond to people.

> If someone strikes you on one cheek, turn to him the other also. If someone takes your cloak, do not stop him from taking your tunic. (Luke 6:29)

What happens when you are insulted or hurt by someone else? Jesus tells us that when someone strikes us on one cheek we are to turn the other cheek. This requires self-control. The natural instinct is to retaliate. We want to get even. The cry of the Spirit, on the other hand, is to turn the other cheek. The Spirit of God in us restrains us and reminds us of God's purpose, keeping us from respond-ing in fleshly anger.

Self-Control and the Use of the Tongue

James tells us that the hardest thing on earth to control is the tongue:

> All kinds of animals, birds, reptiles and creatures of the sea are being tamed and have been tamed by man, 3:8 but no man can tame the tongue. It is a restless evil, full of deadly poison. (James 3:7)

How often I have spoken words that came directly from the flesh. These words have been filled with pride. They have not been helpful for the one who was listening. There have been times when I have even sensed that inner nudge of the Spirit telling me not to speak certain words and yet they still came out of my mouth. He who exercises the fruit of self-control listens to the prompting of the Spirit and carefully weighs his words. Listen to what Paul told the Ephesians:

> (4:29) Do not let any unwholesome talk come out of your mouths, but only what is helpful for build-ing others up according to their needs, that it may benefit those who listen. (4:30) And do not grieve the Holy Spirit of God, with whom you were sealed for the day of redemption. (4:31) Get rid of all bitterness, rage and anger, brawling and slan-der, along with every form of malice. (4:32) Be kind and compassionate to one another, forgiving each other, just as in Christ God forgave you. (Ephesians 4:29-32)

Notice the connection between controlling what came out of their mouths and grieving the Holy Spirit. This connec-tion is significant. There is a relationship between the lack of self-control in the use of our words and grieving the

Holy Spirit. He who controls himself, chooses to listen to the Holy Spirit instead of his flesh. The one who demonstrates the fruit of self-control in his life surrenders to the Holy Spirit in the use of his tongue.

Self-Control and Sexual Passions

In 1 Corinthians 7:7-9 Paul challenges those who were not married to remain unmarried unless they lacked control of their sexual desires:

> (7:7) I wish that all men were as I am. But each man has his own gift from God; one has this gift, another has that. (7:8) Now to the unmarried and the widows I say: It is good for them to stay unmarried, as I am. (7:9) But if they cannot control themselves, they should marry, for it is better to marry than to burn with passion.

Notice that Paul had a particular gift from God in verse 7. God gave him the ability to remain single without the need for a relationship with a member of the opposite sex. The Holy Spirit gave Paul self-control in the area of his sexuality. The Spirit produced this fruit in a special way for Paul to enable him to be devoted fulltime to the ministry of the gospel.

The fruit of self-control is not produced in the same way in all believers. For many believers the Spirit of God does not take away their sexual needs. Instead He gives them a partner with whom those needs can be fulfilled. Self-control is not always about crushing desire or emotion. Some of those passions and desires are legitimate. Paul speaks about the need of widows for companionship and intimacy. For these widows, self-control was to be exercised not by refusing to give in to their basic need of intimacy and companionship but rather by finding a godly context for those needs to be ministered to and expressed.

We must each seek the Lord's direction and guidance in how we deal with the passions, needs and desires. God expected Paul to trust Him for the strength to exercise self-control as a single person. The widows in Corinth were to exercise that control by trusting the Lord for a partner. The exercise of self-control was different for Paul than for the widows but each needed the leading and strength of God to walk in obedience and victory over the flesh.

It is the work of the Spirit of God to enable us to walk in obedience to God by producing the fruit of self-control in our lives. He does so by convicting us of wrong attitudes or desires. He leads us into godly ways of satisfying our passions. He works in us to strip away ungodly attitudes. The Spirit of God in us is working hard to shape us into the image of Christ. As he does so He trains us in this matter of self-control. As we surrender to His leading and rebukes, we grow in maturity and godliness.

For Consideration:

- What is the difference between self-control as a human discipline and the fruit of self-control that Paul speaks about here?
- If self-control is a fruit of God's Spirit, does it require effort on our part? What is the connection between self-control and surrender? What is the

role of God's Spirit in self-control? What is our role?

- How important is self-control in the life of the be-liever? Can we be mature without this fruit in our life?
- What areas of your life need the work of God's Spirit to produce self-control?
- How does the evidence of the fruit of self-control differ from person to person?

For Prayer:

- Take a moment to thank the Holy Spirit for His willingness to produce self-control in your life.
- Ask the Lord to show you if there are areas of your life where you need to demonstrate self-control in a deeper way. Ask the Spirit of God to forgive you for resisting His work in this area of your life.
- Ask God to give you more and more victory over the flesh and its ways. Pray that you would be more sensitive to the teaching and enabling of the Holy Spirit in your life.

CHAPTER 11

FRUIT NOT LAW

Against such there is no law (Galatians 5:23)

As we conclude this brief study I would like to conclude with the words of Paul in verse 23. After speaking in some detail about the fruit of the Spirit, Paul concludes with these words: "Against such there is no law." What does Paul mean by this, and how does it apply to the fruit of the Spirit?

The larger context of Galatians 5 speaks not only about the fruit of the Spirit but also about the fruit of the flesh. Writing in Galatians 5:19-21 Paul describes the fruit of the flesh as follows:

> (19) The acts of the sinful nature are obvious: sexual immorality, impurity and debauchery; (20) idolatry and witchcraft; hatred, discord, jealousy, fits of rage, selfish ambition, dissensions, factions (21) and envy; drunkenness, orgies, and the like. I warn you, as I did before, that those who live like this will not inherit the kingdom of God.

The evil of the sinful nature is obvious all around us. Who among us is not confronted daily with sexual immorality, envy, selfishness or dissensions? We may even feel a struggle in our own hearts to overcome the fruit of the flesh. It was because of this sinful nature that God gave His law. The law was necessary because of sin. Its purpose was to keep law breakers in line with the purpose of God for their society. The problem with the law was that while it showed us what was acceptable before God, it could not change the heart.

Writing in Galatians 5:18, however, Paul told the believers:

> But if you are led by the Spirit, you are not under law.

The way of the law will only bring defeat. Not one of us can measure up to the standard God has set out for us. That is why He has given us His Spirit. The Holy Spirit comes to dwell in the heart of the believer. His goal is to produce in our lives the fruit we have spoken about in this study. He comes to change us from the inside. He works in our heart producing the fruit of love, joy, peace, peace, patience, kindness, goodness, faithfulness, gentleness and self-control.

As the Spirit of God produces His fruit in us, the result is that we begin to walk in harmony with God's ways. He does what the law could never do. He stirs up a new desire in us. He builds the character of Jesus Christ into our lives. We find ourselves responding differently than those around us. The desires of the flesh become repulsive to us. We long to be more like Jesus and find great satisfaction and fulfillment in Him and His purposes for our lives.

As Paul said in Galatians 5:18: "if you are led by the Spirit, you are not under law." In other words, if we are led by the Spirit we will not need the law to guide us for the Spirit will be our Guide. In this study we have been examining the character building work of God's Spirit. If we allow Him, He will shape us into the image of Christ and make us more like Him in every way. He will do this by convicting us of sin (John 16:8) and teaching us how to live and walk with Christ (John 16:13). He will lead us into the fullness of God's purposes. No law could ever do this for us. The law can show us what is right, but it cannot change us. The Spirit of God does both.

When Paul concludes this passage with the words: "against such there is no law," he is telling us that what the Spirit of God is doing in our lives by producing His fruit in us fulfills every purpose of God. To walk in obedience to the Spirit and to surrender to His work is to become all God intends us to be. No court of law would ever find us guilty if we allow the Spirit of God to produce His fruit in us. The Spirit of God will bring us into perfect harmony with the purpose of God.

These words of Paul are a fitting end to this study. To allow the Spirit to produce His fruit in our lives is to walk in harmony with God. The question believers need to ask themselves is: "How can I surrender more to what the Spirit of God is doing in my life?" For only in surrender to Him am I able to walk in obedience to God and all His requirements.

How we need to praise the Lord God for the work of His Spirit. He does not leave us helplessly before the law trying to figure out how we could ever manage to walk in obedience. He takes on the responsibility to change us Himself by dwelling in us and changing us from the inside. He works in our life to produce the character of Christ in us. This is an amazing reality for those who know the Lord Jesus. We are being transformed by the power of God's Spirit who lives in us. He is producing a spiritual fruit in our lives. This fruit is evidence of the Spirit's work and assurance that we belong to God. Those who belong to God are being transformed day by day through this inner character building work of the Spirit.

For Consideration:

- What was the purpose of the Law of God? Did the law enable us to live according to God's standard?
- What is the role of the Holy Spirit? How does He enable us to live as God intends?
- What specific work has the Holy Spirit been doing in your life?
- What is the difference between seeking to follow the law in our own strength and allowing the Spirit of God to produce His fruit in us?

For Prayer:

- Thank the Lord that He has given us His Holy Spirit to enable us to walk in His ways.
- Take a moment to thank the Lord for some particular fruit He has been producing in you. Ask God to show you any areas of your life where you need to surrender more fully to Him.

Light To My Path Book Distribution

Light To My Path (LTMP) is a book writing and distribution ministry reaching out to needy Christian workers in
Asia, Latin America, and Africa. Many Christian workers
in developing countries do not have the resources
necessary to obtain Bible training or purchase Bible study
materials for their ministries and personal encouragement. F. Wayne Mac Leod is a member of Action International Ministries and has been writing these books with a
goal to distribute them to needy pastors and Christian
workers around the world.

To date tens of thousands of books are being used in
preaching, teaching, evangelism and encouragement of
local believers in over sixty countries. Books have now
been translated into a number of languages. The goal is
to make them available to as many believers as possible.

The ministry of LTMP is a faith based ministry and we
trust the Lord for the resources necessary to distribute
the books for the encouragement and strengthening of
believers around the world. Would you pray that the Lord
would open doors for the translation and further distribution of these books?

For more information about Light To My Path Book
Distribution visit our website at www.ltmp.ca.

Made in the USA
Coppell, TX
17 November 2023

24363692R00075